The Mystery of the Sea

Guide to learn to walk on Water

Ina Custers van Bergen

The Mystery of the SEA

Guide to learn to walk on water

Ina Custers van Bergen

Copyright © Ina Cüsters-van Bergen 2015
Illustrations © Ina Custers van Bergen
Translation © Ina Custers van Bergen
Photo Henry Arvidsson http://henryarvidsson.photography/
Book midwife Yoeke Nagel http://yoekenagel.nl/
Editor: Ella Marie

All rights reserved. No part of this book may be reproduced, stored in a retrieval system or transmitted in any form or by any means, electronic, mechanical, photocopying, recording or otherwise, without the prior permission in writing of the copyright owners.

ISBN 978.90.8612.069.7
CC proof 55db155b50278.pdf

Stichting Temple of Starlight publications 2015
Waterwerk 80
3063 HB Rotterdam
The Netherlands

Visit our website;
www.inacusters.com
www.themysteryofthesea.com
www.templeofstarlight.eu
www.axismundiacademy.nl

Sleeping priestesses and magicians
Slumbering in an Eternal Sea,
Between the Dream Lights,
Drifting in the Oceans of Stars,
Are you longing for a Golden Heaven
Kneeling under a honey colored firmament?
Awake, wake up!

Foreword

The world of the Sacred Science (Magic) is a complex one and although there are many writers on various aspects of it most of them are useless simply because the authors have not themselves gone through the rigorous study and discipline that the subject requires.

That is what makes this author different. Here Ina Cüsters-van Bergen knows exactly what she is talking about. She has been fully trained, and has gone through the discipline. She has worked with others and learned with them how to avoid the pitfalls that lie in wait for the unwary. The Sacred Science is a demanding study, it needs time, effort, patience, and dedication. This book will guide you through such a training and although at some time in the future you will need to work with a personal teacher it will ensure you are well prepared and have a better understanding of what will be asked of you.

Think of it as the prerequisite of a highly specialized university course and you would not be far wrong. It can take up to three years and often more, according to how much time you can give to it, to attain a reasonable grasp of this wide ranging subject that has its beginning in distant past of humanity's involvement with worship and belief systems. Taken seriously and followed with dedication this book will open your eyes to a whole new way of understanding that much mis-used word MAGIC.

Dolores Ashcroft-Nowicki
(2007)

Introduction

Do you have the feeling there is 'more'? Do you find yourself in the middle of the 'Is-that-all-there-is' crisis? Maybe kundalini energy has suddenly woken up in you. Or unexpected meaningful events happen and strange images bubble up before your inner eye from the depths of your unconscious mind.

Are you curious to investigate them? Do you dare step through the Gates of Wonder? This does not mean that your quest needs to be for Eastern Wisdom; there is a Western Way, called Hermetics which seamlessly complements our Western cultural roots. Waking up to the 'Otherworld' is a sign that your inner self wants to develop. Your soul wants to blossom, your heart desires to investigate this wondrous reality. The ancient Greeks called it *Metanoia,* which was a soul search through the 'under-spirit', a search for the Alchemical Gold of the soul. Descending into the depths of your subconscious mind, you arrive in the mythological layers of your consciousness. This part of your mind is underestimated yet important. During an 'Is-that-all-there-is' crisis, parts of these mythological layers can erupt into your conscious mind. Meaningful events happen, images surface; supernatural and divine. Integrate them and you will walk the road of transformation into wholeness.

Great genii from Western history practiced this mental alchemy, among them Carl Gustav Jung. Our increasing rationalization causes us to fear this natural process of spiritual awakening. The knowledge about the healing effects of *Metanoia* and the accompanying spiritual training to harvest its fruits, are at risk of being lost. Within the New Age movement people call this a 'kundalini crisis', they diagnose themselves as hypersensitive, HSP or psychic. They are left with mind-boggling questions about their experiences and an incapability to deal with them.

Myths are of the key to bringing this internal process to fruition. Without the accompanying myths you become uprooted, and don't develop a connection to the spiritual legacy of our ancestors that lays dormant deep inside your soul. The subconscious mind communicates in a symbolic language. You would recognize this from your dreams. The message appears bizarre and baffling, as our natural connection to the 'Otherworld' has been disrupted. Western meditation works with symbols that train you to communicate with your subconscious mind and translate the dream world of images into inner knowledge. This causes a flowing river of meaning connecting the unconscious mind to everyday life.

This book tells the story of Jason Adams, a journalist who is shattered by an 'Otherworld' experience. It tells about his struggle to make sense of his experiences and his quest to get to the bottom of a deeper reality, which is causal for our everyday experiences.

In this book I use mythical symbol language. Some words have a capital letter. These words are doors to inner experiences and realizations. There is a distinction between the earth under your feet and the Earth Element, which is a symbol for the ability to manifest your life's wishes. There is a contrast between lighting a fire and the Fire Element which is a symbol for passion and vitality. The water of the ocean differs from the Water of the Ocean, because the latter is symbolic of the vastness of the unconscious mind. To get a breath of air differs from the Air Element which is a metaphor for your mental abilities.

Through this story I hope to create some sympathy for the *Metanoia* process, to help people open themselves up to spiritual development and start training this ability which leads to a rich harvest of inner wisdom, that you can apply in your wider life.

INA CUSTERS VAN BERGEN

Contents

Foreword 6

Introduction 7

Contents 9

1. Lapis Sancti Magi 13
2. The Eye of the Winged Human Being 35
   Great Kabbalistic Cross 58
3. The Search for Dry Land 71
   The Primordial Hill - meditation 108
4. The Water Spells 115
   Ebb 115
   The Winding Waterway 123
   Flood 132
   The Water Spells 132
   The Ship of Stars 145
5. The Dragons under the Mountain 155
   Everything of Value is Vulnerable 155
   The Secret of Myrddin 181
6. The Wizards War 187
   The Disposable Truth 198
   Pulver Pelagiieremitae 208

    The Paradise Garden..210

    The Spirit of the Deep 220

7. The Dancing Beauty.. 225

    Awaken the Sleepers!.. 237

    Ignite your Interior Stars! 243

    Ora et Labora... 248

    The Spirit of the Deep 252

    The Mystery of the Sea 270

How to proceed?.. 274

Ina Custers van Bergen 276

The Temple of High Magic.. 279

    References 281

DIRECTION IS RELATIVE,

WITHDRAWAL CAN BRING PROGRESS

BY REVERSING THE GOAL.

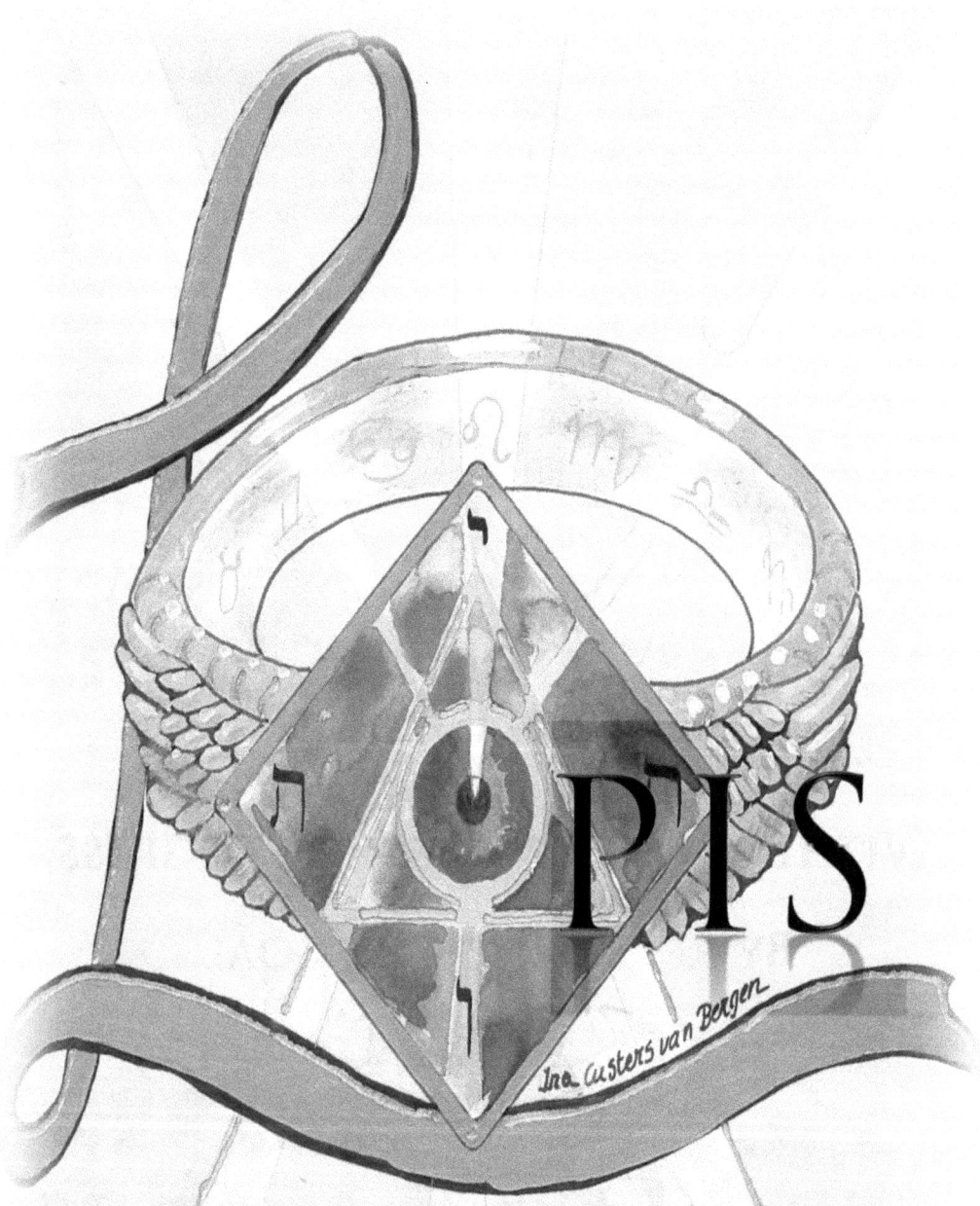

1

LAPIS SANCTI MAGI

London 1980

The weekend workshop is almost over. What a fantastic adventure it was. Only with a long and shared history it is possible to experience such an extraordinary feeling of connectedness with people you hardly know within a weekend. I think that this is only possible among members of the Family of Ancients. With sadness in my heart I pack my clothes and carefully tuck away the papers with the teachings of past weekend. The texts remind me of the weekend's events: the enchanting beauty, the echoing voices, and the personal affection in the twinkling lights of the eyes. I check my flight ticket and look at the schedule of the bus which will take me to the airport. A last half hour, and then it is time to go.

Carefully I fold the precious clothing that I have had especially made for these events. I pick up the velvet pouch to store my jewelry. I don't pack them in my suitcase, but keep them safe in my hand luggage. I pick up my necklace, and search for my ring.

The ring and its box are missing. Strange, I tucked it away safely yesterday. A cold panic creeps over me, while I check all the logical places. Not on the desk, not in my handbag.

I start to search the illogical places, on my knees crawling over the dusty floor. My arm just fits under the heavy bed. My fingertips feel for minuscule subjects that might be lying there for years. No ring. Stress... I pull the sheets from the bed, turn the mattress upside down, look and bend down to feel every inch of the floor. The ring is gone.

"I am sure that I put it away in its box. This is strange. Was I mistaken? When the ring fell on the ground, where did its box go?" Again I kneel down and search under the desk. Nothing. I take my mobile telephone to use it as a torch. I lie down flat on the floor and carefully grope for the ring: but it stays missing.

A knock on the door. "Melusine, are you ready?" Eagle is waiting. "We need to go; otherwise we'll miss the bus."

"I lost my ring."

"How is that possible? You were wearing it an hour ago, during the last session," Eagle says with a light irritation in his voice.

"I don't get it at all. It must be here in my room. I turned everything upside down, but it simply disappeared into thin air," I answer, being on the verge of tears.

"Ask at the reception desk for the staff to search for it when they clean the room. They can send it on when they find it", Eagle answers. "We need to say our goodbyes to everyone and go now."
Reluctantly, I leave the hotel room to make the arrangements that Eagle suggested and see the elderly lady who organized the entire weekend to say thanks. "Tethys, I have lost my ring," I tell her.

Tethys bends over, squeezes her eyes while she concentrates. I tell her about my search and she listens to the details carefully. "It is a charged ring, Melusine", she says. "Such objects of power have their own lives. They search for owners and journey when someone else needs them. It is similar to the missing pen or the disappearance of clothes hangers from your closet, or being left with one half of a pair of socks. Your ring has left and it is probably on a mission to find a new owner. You are entering a new phase. There is someone who will need the powers of this ring."
She continues, "Unexpected disappearances or appearances of this type of charged objects are a sign of rising energy and preparing the next phase of your development. If the ring has not returned to you within a Moon cycle, you should let it go. Bless the person who will find your ring, because he or she will need help. These power objects release a storm in someone's life and will cause someone to change forever."
With a deep sigh I bow my head, say goodbye...

Sleeping priestesses and magicians
Slumbering in an Eternal Sea,
Between the dream lights drifting in the Oceans of Stars,
Longing for a Golden Heaven

And a honey colored firmament;
Awake, wake up!

I call out to you, continue the Great Work.
Follow me; follow the voice of the Lady of the Lake.
The tide is flood
And the Great Ocean is illuminated by the Rising Sun.
I awaken you to continue the Great Work;
Awaken to heal the planet,
To re-ignite the Earthlight,
To feed the bee folk with milk and honey.

*****

The alarm goes off. Half sleeping Jason gropes for the right button to silence the clock. He sits upright and feels his head. A pulsing headache. Too much drinking. His head feels like being hit by a hammer. He turns over. The place next to him is empty. The half opened wardrobe shows the remnants of a nocturnal quarrel.

Slowly waking up, the anger and powerlessness fall over him. The rebuke that he is hardly home. He can't understand it. He is fighting for his career. *I am working overtime off to become a skilled professional. I need to travel by car, to far destinations, conquer traffic jams and when I finally arrive home, I am always blamed*, he thinks.

Her constant reprimands: "You are seldom at home, you don't share your feelings, I hardly know who you are, and when you are with me you are always tired."

I am squeezed like a lemon. That is what you have to do when you want to make a career nowadays, and live in a beautiful home," Jason grumbles silently. *All day long, I listen to the misery of others. At the end of the day, I crave rest and most certainly not for difficult conversations about our relationship.*

For months now, Jason has returned home exhausted. He has just enough energy to hit the button of the remote control. Food, rest, sleep and early rising. Something gnaws deep inside, but he simply lacks time to investigate it. But it is something essential which feels fundamentally wrong. She is right about that. But what?

He sits upright now, headache. *Hangover,* he thinks while he holds both his hands against his throbbing temples. He stumbles to the bathroom, takes a paracetamol and steps in the shower.

Where did she go? Is she at her mothers, or did she go to a friend? Does she see someone else? Jason gasps at this thought; a flame of jealousy blazes throughout his entire body. He hears the soft sound of paws on the lino and a friendly meow. His cat enthusiastically pads towards him. Purring Tiger pushes his head against his leg, hoping to get fed when Jason finishes his morning ritual. Tiger's love sticks to his legs in the shape of wet hair.

"Yes boy, I'll be downstairs in a minute." Jason combs his hair, sweeps away the last remnants of shaving foam and walks thoughtfully after the enthusiastic Tiger, who already sits purring before the kitchen door. Sighing Jason prepares his breakfast, without being hungry at all.

He looks out from the window. The weather is as grey as his mood. Drops slowly run down from the glass and the landscape is shrouded in a thick mist. Now alone, he does not have a goal. He does not feel like cleaning up the mess of her rash departure.

What did I dream last night? Paracetamol is incapable of curing the hangover. His memory returns in rags. An underground ocean. A tunnel running through a mountain. Spiraled corridors connecting the surface with the dark deep. Strange drawings on the walls and ceilings. Honeycombs. Bee's humming and the splashing of water.

Coffee is ready. The chattering noise of the coffee machine hammers his brain. Coffee to wipe away the painful mist. His goal for today needs to be decided. *I will leave the city; I need to be out of this situation for a while.* Jason decides to take his car and drive to Amsterdam. That will distract him from his misery.

He pulls on his thick coat. It is cold outside and wet. He steps in his car and drives to the highway, through the thick mist. Great foggy clouds hang low over the balding trees, a typical late autumn landscape. Thick clouds float like wads of cotton wool in between bushes and trees by the roadside. Silhouettes of a herd of horses in the mist. He is almost alone on this road. It is still early on Saturday morning. *What the hell am I doing on this gleaming road in this grey weather?*

The fog thickens. It is the only thing he sees in the headlights. Dull orbs of oncoming traffic. Slowly he arrives in Amsterdam. From the mist the bike-riders appear unexpectedly, dinging their bells in warning. The drifting ships in the canals look like dark silently floating coffins. In the fog, lanterns cast a mysterious golden light with coronas. Everything reflects itself in the grey waters. A watery sun struggles to break through the clouds and turns the landscape into a faint yellow.

The city awakens. It is a challenge to steer the car over the small bridges and find a parking space beside the canals. He has almost arrived at the Waterlooplein flea market. Jason loves to browse through old bric-a-brac searching for something special. It is always fun to browse through the clutter, to find hidden treasures. He loves antique handmade stuff. It has been ages that he has had the time to do this.

He walks in between the stalls, lifting objects here and there to take a closer look. A wooden telescope on a tripod, with messing edges. A copper coal-scuttle. An antique hanging clock with a set of weights. A stall with antique cameras, exhibited on a tattered Persian carpet. A booth with hats and caps, demonstrated on the bald decapitated heads of manikins. Copper trumpets silently strung from the roof of the stall, awaiting a second life.

Next to a stall with original paintings, there is a salesman selling second hand jewelry. Under glass in a flat wooden box is a strange ring in a smaller case.

"Can I see this ring?" Jason asks. The golden setting holds a star sapphire. In the gold are engraved strange letters and symbols. Jason takes the ring in his hands and gets confused. A strong disturbing energy radiates from the ring. His heart starts to vibrate. "How much is it?" Jason asks as neutrally as possible. The ring is burning in the palm of his hand.

It is much more expensive then Jason planned to spend on himself. But he has to have it. *It is extraordinary*, he thinks as he turns the ring over and studies it. The salesman gives him the ring's jewel box. It is made of bone. The lit has unknown signs engraved in the metal. The trader puts the ring in its box. Jason tucks the package safely away in his inner coat pocket. It is time to Google the meaning of the ring's symbols. He walks over the small bridges back to his car. Bumping over the unequal pavement he returns home.

Back in his own street, his heart sinks. The memory of yesterday evening fills his mind. Joan was so terribly angry. Not like anything Jason had seen before from her. His mobile telephone rings. He tries to guard his heart from emotions, but her message hits him like a punch to the stomach. She speaks quickly. She wants to be on her own for a while, to evaluate her life, her work, and her life with him. She will stay at her mothers'. At first to rest and then to think about her future.

He turns the lock of his front door, walks to the couch and slumps down. *What do I want for myself?* he thinks. *Do I really live?* His days were like walking a treadmill, stressed until completely exhausted. Never experiencing any pleasure.

I write 'news' about events where some idiot compares the length of his tie with an even more-important idiot. It is not news... I just feed a propaganda machine, everything is predetermined. No critical journalism, but articles for money. News to entertain, not to inform, but to cover up. Is that all there is? House, a car, a wife, no kids. A wife? No, maybe that chapter has just ended, because she walked away in anger.

His jaws tighten. His telephone rings. A colleague invites him for "a network opportunity." It is the last thing he needs right now. Receptions, where you dress up, shake hands with bosses, collect quick information and lobby. *This is not what I need.* His thoughts rush around the subject and he answers with a sigh:

"Yes that is excellent, I will send you an invitation later this evening and we will fix a date."

Then he remembers the box in his pocket. He takes it out and places it on the table. A strange sound comes from behind the windows. A bee is trapped behind curtains trying to escape. He opens the curtains, but he does not see any insect.

He picks up the jewel box. *What are these strange symbols on the case?* He opens it and stares at the ring. The salesmen said the stone was a star sapphire. The square gem is set in a unique way in the golden setting. In the metal are engraved symbols and at both sides of the ring a pair of wings are depicted. He wonders about the style. It reminds him of a coat of arms. The jewel has style and Jason tries to imagine how it will fit with his cuffs. It will look impressive at special events when his power suit is required.

He holds the stone to the light. Suddenly a star with six rays shoots from the ring. In the ring's deeper structure a triangle appears. Inside the triangle he suddenly sees an eye. The rays of the star flash from the eye's iris. *Wow, that is beautiful. What would be the meaning of the signs around it? And of the strange symbols on the casket of bone.*

He opens his tablet and quickly beat keywords on the screen. He types the search word 'symbols', and looks at pages full with strange signs.

This is just the beginning of his search. Jason asks himself; *who would order such a ring to be made? It is completely clear to him, that this is no factory work; this is a unique piece of handicraft.*

In the inside of the ring there is engraved a proverb: "Ora et Labora". Jason types the words into the search engine and immediately finds a hit. The maxim comes from a Latin motto which meant 'pray and work.' *So the ring has a spiritual meaning.* He takes a deep breath. Google has let him down. He is looking in the right direction, but he does not know how to proceed.

Jason shuts off the tablet. With hardly any clues he has no idea how to unravel the meaning of the ring's symbols. His mobile phone bleeps; an automatic reminder for the evening's dance party. *This will be no fun at all without Joan. On the other hand, it is better than sitting on the sofa sulking.* He makes a quick decision. He calls a few friends. Simple distraction always helps, dancing is enjoyable. So he picks his clothes for an evening of dancing.

*****

Late Sunday evening and I am still working. Driven and concentrated I type in the lessons that I am preparing for this weekend. I think how to present my program this time.

At midnight I suddenly fall quiet, become alert because of a subtle change of energy around me. A silence fills the atmosphere and my thoughts become still. I recognize this feeling immediately. This is the sensation I get, when something important is about to happen. The hair on the back of my neck stands upright and I feel a strange energy rushing through my body.

I leave the computer and go to my meditation room. I light the contact candle, poor some incense grains on a charcoal and start a deep relaxation. I direct my awareness to the inside and concentrate on my inner senses. As if they are antennae, I listen to their messages and submerge in waves of inner knowing...

Strong thrilling energy transfers itself into images and words. Before my inner eye a staircase appears; a road that takes me downwards to an ancient past. The more I concentrate, the images become more solid and precise. My footsteps echo on the stone. The way downwards is lit by smoking torches that hang in iron holders from the walls.

I take one of the torches and descend. I feel excited when this happens. This is always a new adventure. I descend the spiral shaped path; regress in time and back into history. Deeper into the past; a downward spiral into an infinite depth.

I have reached the most ancient parts of the spiral shaped staircase. Here the steps are completely worn by thousands of feet. I arrive at a wall of irregular shaped boulders. With a proficient craftsmanship they are hewn out and fit exactly. I arrive at a weathered wooden gate. It has characteristic gnarls. Time has caused cracks in the ledges. This is where the stairway leads me. There is a door-knocker. I knock three times on the double doors, and recite the passwords to get access:

I ask access to the Holy City,
Built on an island in the Cosmic Ocean:
Open to me, Temple of Lights,

Sculptured from Lapis Lazuli stone,
Raised for the rites of Magicians and Priests.

House where the incantations for Heaven and Earth resound.
No evil can enter this sacred place,
It is encircled and protected by the Web of Light.

The double doors open and I am greeted by a guardian. He is well built, dark skinned and clothed in a scaled leather tunic. He wears leather trousers, boots and holds a sword. The doors open to a night-soaked landscape, a beach between land and sea. I greet him, he is a dear friend: "Good to see you, Leo." I nod and smile at him.

I sniff the salty air while I admire the landscape: it has a surrealistic beauty. The evening sky is deep blue. The sun has set and the orange afterglow is still to be seen at my left side in the west. The colors of the sunset reflect in the mirror of the waters. An island is visible at the far end. A mountain range lights up purple in the evening air. Above it, in eerie green, the polestar appears. As the first stars emerge, the lights are lit on the island.

I walk towards a wooden ship that lies anchored at the quay. A primitive mast holds a sail, on which is pictured a red rose. The mast is supported and kept upright by thick braided cords. Leo guides me to the floating wooden plank bridge. I walk over the wobbling gang plank and climb aboard the ship. In the boat are seated fourteen rowers. As soon as I am seated on one of the simple wooden benches, the rowers lean into their oars and the ship slowly moves away from the shore.

I enjoy the journey. Beautiful colors grow in intensity, while the night slowly falls. There are the sounds of splashing waves and the drops of salty water from the oars.

A wind tucks my hair and my hands become sticky by the salty air. It is not far to go, the boat trip takes about half an hour and then I land on the island. I set foot at the shore of the old city, together with Leo. I am curious why the Old Ones have called me back to this place. I look forward to meeting the members of the Family again and embrace them.

I draw my mantle tightly around me. The wind is fresh. Fortunately I don't have to go far. I can see the contours of the familiar pyramid shaped building in front of me. Fireplaces before the entrance illuminate the building. When I walk up the stairs, I greet the two guards at the door. They open the portals for me and bow deep. Long purple robes hang ready for my use.

I go to the entrance hall and change, then cross the big hall and walk to my seat in the North. In the middle of the space stands a black cubical stone, decorated with white linen.

I connect myself with the forces behind me. I feel how they flow through me. My body reacts immediately with great heat; I feel the familiar tingling of the energy rushing through me. Through my spine, a strong flow of power starts to rise. I concentrate on my environment and see my colleagues, who begin to manifest as they take their seats. Smoke appears and from it forms the trusted face of Eagle. It has been a long time since we have seen each other in this way. There are so few of us, of the Old Blood, awake and in incarnation. What a privilege that we are allowed to come together, to awaken the next generation of the Old Family.

I walk to the altar in the middle of the room, ignite the altar light and set fire to a charcoal with incense. It fills the entire space with sweet smelling smoke. I take the candle flame and use it to ignite a circle of flames. I concentrate at the water on the altar and sprinkle the entire room to purify it.

Now Dindrane walks to the altar and puts a clay figure of a baby on the stone. Michael approaches it with his flaming sword and ignites the central light. Eagle makes a hole in the clay and carefully inserts the symbol of a beating heart. Then we bow towards each other. The space is loaded with a tangible energy, comparable with an approaching thunderstorm. I raise my hands and make contact. The energy gathers like a ball between my hands. I bring my left hand down and hold it over the clay baby. Then I feel the energy like a lightning flash rushing through me, striking the artwork underneath my hand.

We gather in the center of the room and watch how our focused thoughts create a shape in a rising nebula that slowly evaporates from the clay baby. It draws together like a ball, an energy field that explodes in a cascade of hundreds of lights, each of them erupts like fireworks. From the center, the sparks rise upwards and splash in all directions, filling the entire space. When we break the circle, they float in all directions and fly away in the night. I look at the others, satisfied: the work is completed. I smile, we salute and each of us returns back to the place where their physical bodies rest.

The way back is always quicker than the journey out. When I have climbed the stairs and am back in my meditation room, I notice the temperature has dropped. I return to my body, stiffened by the cold. What time is it? I have been away for hours; it is deep in the night.

I rub my limbs to help my muscles to become supple again, move my head in all directions to let the stiffness disappear. I notice that it has become too late to work further at the preparation for the lesson. I close my work with a glass of honey wine.

*****

The pounding music is already heard of miles away from the entrance of the club. A long line of people stands waiting at the door. Jason, Robin and Rudolph line up at the end of the queue. Jason has briefly informed them about Joan's departure. He told them not to ask questions, but to simply to go out and have fun. Distraction is what he really needs.

The entire day remains fuzzy and cold. Everyone is wrapped up in warm coats. Little clouds of steam rise up from the warm breath in the cold air. Jason stamps his feet and retreats deeper in his coat to keep himself warm. Fortunately, the line in front of him shrinks quickly. Approaching the pay desk, the music becomes louder; it makes him happy. He walks through the door and arrives in a surrealistically lit dancehall. Colored spotlights shine on the dancers: purple, yellow, red.

Rudolph pats Jason at the back. "This is what we guys need sometimes, laddie. When life becomes tough, there is always the gang and the smell of sweat and beer."

White shirts light up in fluorescent purple against the dark background. The atmosphere is heavily loaded. Smiling women stand packed together in sexy dresses, finding a way to the bar through the crowd. Jason studies them top to bottom. He divides them into two categories; sweet and beautiful. When the D.J. announces the next dance, all the arms raise and the crowd prepares for the coming dance. Couples swing their hips together on the beat, while judging the other, watching and being watched. Jason smiles to the lady in the shiny dress, who puts her arm on his shoulder. He enjoys the enthusiasm the D.J. can to raise from his glaring stage.

The beat uplifts his mood. This is what he needs; an adventure with the boys. He forgets everything and swings, moves, senses his body, his muscles, becomes one with the drums, feels the rhythm going through his body. His feet move at the pulse of the beat. The drums penetrate his entire body. A boost of energy shoots up through his spine. Dancing is ecstasy, his heart becomes bigger and it appears to open even further on the rise and fall of the movements. His breath quickens; throughout his body involuntary movements start to stir. The energy takes over. This no longer feels comfortable. What is the matter? His heartbeat quickens and a wave of fear spreads though his body. *What is happening?* He breaks into a cold sweat. He gets dizzy and nauseous. He staggers to the side and grasps a table top to prevent him from falling. Still the movements are taking over his muscles.

I don't understand why I feel this sick so unexpectedly. He breathes heavily.

Jason flees the dance hall and takes a seat in the corridor to catch his breath. Robin comes towards him and asks whether he is okay. "No, definitely not," Jason admits sighing.

"Maybe it is time to go home?" Rudolph considerately calls a cab for him. Jason picks up his jacket from the cloakroom and gets in the taxi. In the car he collects his thoughts. *Maybe this is all too much right now. The pressure at work, the argument with Joan, her departure. Maybe it is just a backlash from the beer, from being overtired, the stress and emotions caused me to hyperventilate.*

Everything returns back to normal again. He breathes deeply. The best thing to do now is to go home and sleep, tomorrow is another day.

Home again. But this time it feels different. The silence catches him off guard when he enters his dark house. Tiger immediately comes running towards him. "Tiger, boy, you haven't had your evening meal yet." Guilty, Jason goes to the kitchen to feed the hungry cat. Then he falls into bed and into in a restless sleep. He wakes up, and stretches out but instead of the soft body of Joan; he feels the warm fur of Tiger, who has claimed the empty pillow.

He falls asleep again… Footsteps in a blearing space and a penetrating buzzing of bees. Loudly, as if a swarm of insects circles around his head. Images appear around him. A strange room decorated with sea horses. High marble pillars support the ceiling. His footsteps echo, when he walks through a long corridor. He notices the rosacea on the ceiling…

…A woman appears, dressed in long robes, a hood drawn over her head. She wears strange jewelry and carries an incense burner. She throws grains of incense on the burning charcoals and a coiling smoke rises. The colors change and a strange passage appears. It is as if a different dimension appears within the room. The space is encircled by a wall of flames. Jason looks through the dimensions and feels like he is falling. A ride on a rollercoaster downwards at an increasing acceleration. A sensation of weightlessness. Adrenaline pumps and the speed keeps increasing. His heart pounds and the involuntary movements start. A throbbing energy at the bottom of his spine. Heat rises slowly. Pain, tears, fears, love and old memories alternate. His body starts to shake. Hot as if in fever. Lights flash around him.

It is not a dream. He is awake. He breaths fast. In the darkness of the bedroom the well-known outlines of the objects become alive. Lights. But nothing is to be seen. His body temperature is normal and everything in the bedroom is exactly the way it should be. *It is not normal to have this kind of nightmare.* Tiger still sleeps on his pillow uninterested and grumbles softly when Jason lies down again.

*****

There is an atmosphere of excited tension. The doorbell rings every few minutes and people start to arrive. Most of the visitors greet each other enthusiastically and exchange news. Some arrive for the first time, look around attentively to see what is going on and take a 'wait and see' attitude, while they sit on a bar stool and almost stir the bottom out of their coffee cup.

In the big hall, the team is busy preparing the meeting. The chairs are put in a semi-circle in three double rows. At the open side of the half circle stands a high seat with lion's paws for arms. Dindrane arranges a bouquet of red roses and white lilies in a small high vase. Luke greets the visitors that enter into the antechamber enthusiastically. He enters into the big hall to make the final touches by decorating a corner with beautiful crystals. Leo lights some candles and dims the light to enhance the room's atmosphere. Gabriella is nervous. Her senses stand at the ready and intuitively she knows what is about to happen. She takes a glass and a carafe of water and sets it at the right place.

Now everyone is welcomed and the team withdraws and changes clothes. Calming music is played in the background and Wolf sounds the bells. The light is dimmed. Slowly four people enter into the room walking carefully to the rhythm of the music. All are dressed in long robes, their faces hidden in their hoods. Each of them carries an object. Wolf holds a staff, Luke a flat dish, Michael a sword and Gabriella a chalice. Slowly and with dignity they walked to their places. When they arrive the warm sound of a gong fills the entire space. It is the signal for me to enter.

The double doors open and I enter the candle lit room bare foot. I feel the soft sounds of music touch my soul. The hall is filled with known and unknown people. I experience the energy rushing through me and see how my true being starts to overshadow my outer appearance. The powers rush through me and start filling the atmosphere.

The entire hall becomes noiseless when I pass through it. I walk to the stage, to the high seat with the lions paws. I climb the stairs and carefully lift the skirt of my golden robes. Wolf reaches me his hand, while I lean on the large laurel branch that I carry in my left hand. With dignity I climb the stairs. My long blue silk scarf covers my hair; it drops forward while I climb the steps. The decorating small golden stars flicker in the candle light. My four assistants are focused and concentrated. I look deep into their eyes and see the powers rise that erupt from a deep inner concentration.

I stand upright, look through the hall and connect myself with the my most ancient part. Clearly I feel how my Sphere of Sensation[1] fills the entire space and from the root of my spine a golden force rises, pulsating, beating. When I speak, my voice has become deep and pealing, it fills the entire space. Before my feet stands an iron cauldron filled with glowing charcoal. Wolf throws some of the laurel leafs on the coal and fragrant fumes start to rise. I smell the spicy leafs and then the words follow. They come automatically as if they have a life of their own. They stream through me, because not I myself, but the Source of Wisdom speaks.

From the Point of Love,
Directly from the Heart of the One
My love streams to the hearts of all of you.
All Words of Power are spoken with Love
From the center of the Wisdom of the Will.
Our intention is guided to that goal,
That all Masters know and serve.

---

[1] Within the Hermetic Mystery Tradition we use a vocabulary of our own. The 'Sphere of Sensation' is in Eastern Mysticism often called the 'aura'.

From the core of the center of the Soul of Humanity
Runs the power that seals the Doors against all evil.
The Light returns to the world!
From the place where Knowledge and Word are one,
Love, Power and Wisdom flow out to all people,
They guide our thoughts and our acts.
On behalf of those who perceive the One face to face,
I bring thee greetings!

"The summoning has taken place. Last night I went to the Old City where we joined our forces in a Great Working. The Working has been extremely successful. The effect is a wakeup call in all directions to those people who are ripe and sensitive enough to pick up the signal. Shortly I expect the first people to contact us, through email, telephone and in all possible ways, in ways we can hardly imagine."

My message causes a buzz in the audience. People start to talk to each other and exchange questions and answers. Wolf waits a little while and then he knocks with his staff on the floor. The crowd silences immediately.

"Are there people that have questions?" I look around and make eye contact. All faces look happy and appear to look forward to the coming events.

"Good, than we can now proceed with our normal work. I would like to ask the people on the cardinal directions to hand out the papers and I will explain what we will be practicing during today's' training."

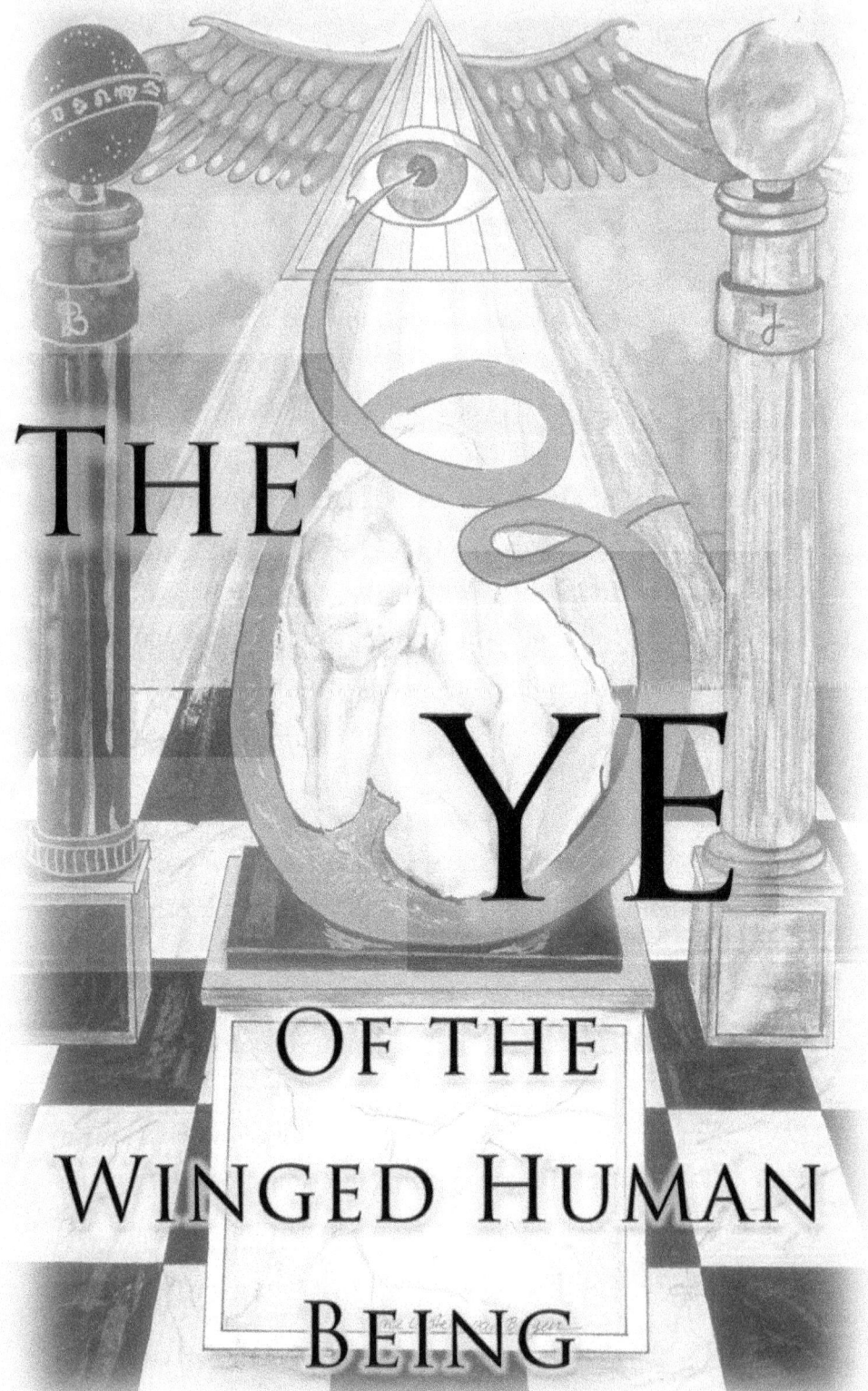

The Eye Of the Winged Human Being

2

THE EYE OF THE WINGED HUMAN BEING

When Jason reawakens, everything appears to be normal again. No evidence is left of the nightly turbulence. He is looking forward to an ordinary Sunday. He loves to go to the country and spend time on his bike, working out and sweating. But now he sighs, rain is pouring down the windows. Today the only option to work out will be the gym. He starts to gather his sport outfit. Would one of his friends be willing to join him? A round of telephone calls ends without results.

But his friend, William Smith, is at home. William is not a sportsman but a book collector. Jason decides to visit William after the workout. It has been a while since they have seen each other. Then, he gets an idea. Jason decides to take the ring with him to show it to William. Maybe he can help him to figure out the meaning of the inscriptions in the jewel.

He quickly collects his belongings and picks up the box of bone with the ring inside. He opens it once again, wondering about the symbols. Then he hits the road.

After half an hour's drive, Jason arrives at the small cottage where William lives. His house is very close to the sea. He lives at the first floor of a former fisher's home. Jason rings the bell while he looks upwards, to the window at the first floor. William appears waving, opens the window and throws down the key of the front door. His legs are too old and too tired to climb the stairs unnecessarily. Jason opens the lock of the cracking door. He feels some advertisement leaflets block the door. He pushes a bit to open it and removes the paper mountain by picking up the leaflets. He takes them with him upstairs. His feet step on the hairy hall rug, which is fastened with rails to the stairs. He greets William who is waiting on the first floor, leaning heavily on the banisters.

"I have collected your mail for you," says Jason.

"Thank you, that helps me a lot," William answers.

"How are you doing?" Jason asks.

"My old bones are hurting. The doctor has given me a new prescription, but I don't feel any better. It is an annoying affliction," he answers.

William shambles inside and Jason wonders again about the huge compilation of extraordinary articles William has managed to collect. Walls with the strangest collection of books he has ever seen combined with a great variety of curious handmade... what are they? Objects of art? William has always been eccentric. Some years ago Williams's house had to be renovated and he still speaks about the event that caused all of his belongings to be replaced. He is still searching for various items since they did not return to their proper places.

Jason takes a seat at the great wooden table in the middle of the room and looks around, while William shuffles to the kitchen to make coffee.

"How old are you, William?" Jason asks.

"Ah, I did not get younger," William answers. "I will be seventy shortly."

"Will you be celebrating that?" Jason asks.

"No way, there is nobody interested in such an event," William grumbles.

William is turning into an old groaner, Jason thinks. He has probably more pain from his afflictions than he admits.

After talking about health issues and the weather, Jason mentions the ring.

"William, look what I found on Waterloo Square yesterday. I am so curious to hear your opinion about it." Jason takes the box from his pocket and slides it over the table to William.

"Let me put on my glasses first," William answers. He takes his reading glasses and puts them at the edge of his nose. Carefully he lifts the box. He taps on the surface and listens to the sound. "That is bone," he says. "It is hand cut, beautifully made!" The old hands shake slightly and William upholds the box up to catch daylight. "Those messing fittings have been decorated with a purpose in mind," William says. "Some of the inscriptions are blurred but they hold a symbolic meaning."

William touches the lid with his fingers and says: "That copper sphere with those rays represents the sun." He counts the rays. "Twelve? That makes sense." Now he switches on a reading lamp and takes a loupe to study the details.

"Look here, originally there were signs inscribed, but they are almost gone. And the lock, strangely...it has the shape of some kind of head with eyes, although you don't notice this at first sight."

William now opens the box and sees the ring. "Ghee, yes I can imagine why you wanted to have it," he says surprised. He carefully picks up the ring and examines it closely.

"What are those signs that are inscribed in the rim?" Jason asks while bending forward. "In the edge is written, 'Ora et Labora,' but all the rest is abracadabra to me."

"Then you are heading for the right direction," William laughs. "Because it looks like a ritual ring. First of all this thing has been specially made; this type of jewelry is not made in mass production."

Jason nods, he had come to the same conclusion. "But do you recognize the tokens that are inscribed around the stone?"

"Ehh...yes ehh...," William hesitates. He upholds the ring under the lamp and armed with loop and reading glasses he moves the ring up and down.

"Those tokens around the stone; that is Hebrew. They are the letters Yod, Heh, Vav and Heh, the four letters of the Tetragrammaton."

"What is that?" Jason asks.

"The Tetragrammaton is the unpronounceable Name of God. The four letters are placed around the stone. The engravings surrounding the gem represent the Eye of God. From the Eye spring six rays. This is highly symbolic abracadabra." William looks Jason straight in the eyes.

"And those other tokens?" Jason asks.

"The stone represents the Eye of God, in between two golden wings. You can also find these types of wings in Egyptian symbolism, for example in pictures of the Winged Solar Disk. But, in other cultures winged symbols were also pictured. They always indicate a connection with something 'heavenly,' something not of this world." William rises and stretches his stiff muscles. He shuffles in the direction of the large bookcases. "I have a book in which this type of symbolism is explained," he says. "But I hope I can find it quickly, since they renovated my house some things have disappeared or became invisible."

His fingers move along the shelves. He picks out a small booklet and walks back to the table. It is a book with a lot of colored illustrations. He flips through the leaves and shows Jason pages full of winged symbols. Not only a winged sun, but also a winged lion, a winged bull, a winged horse, a winged snake, a winged griffin and a lot more excellent pictures of art from ancient cultures.

"And what do you think of the tokens in the outer edge?" Jason asks.

"Those are Astrological signs," William says. "That is not my expertise. Every zodiac sign is depicted by a hieroglyph and those tokens resemble these signs, as also the ones engraved at the bottom of the stone."

"Where?" Jason asks.

"Here, look," William says and he turns the ring upside down so that Jason can take a good look at the gold underneath the stone. Indeed, there are seven symbols that Jason completely overlooked six in a circle and a seventh in the center.

William picks up the box once again and explores. He opens the lit and studies the lining of the box. It is a faded purple velvet fabric that lost color in the ravages of time.

"In some way the bottom does not fit with the rest," William says. He thoughtfully gazes into the box, feeling with his fingers. "Can I pick into it with a knife?" he asks while he shuffles towards the kitchen and starts pottering around in the kitchen drawer.

Jason feels the tension in his shoulders and his heart beats heavily in his chest, while he studies the inside of the box.

William returns with a paring knife. He carefully places it in the bottom, lifts it and finds a leaf of paper underneath. A text is written on it. Jason and William stare at the half blurred letters and start to decipher the message:

Lapis Sancti Magi:
The Eye of the Winged Human Being opens itself slowly in you,
The Sacred Fire awakens in you,
On the pulsations of the Winged Snake.
Ora et Labora!

They look at each other flabbergasted. "Look at the note," Jason says. William unfolds the leaflet. It is a piece of paper that obviously came out of an old typing machine. The backside was used to make a sketch. The colors are gone and the paper has clearly been wet, but the drawing is still clear. It looks as if it served as a design for the ring.

On the backside there's an outline and a sloppy quick handwriting. Also here the letters leaked through the paper on the place where the water went through. But it is possible to read the note:

This way I want it to look, with the four Hebrew letters encircling the stone, the magical motto in the inside margin and the entire [....]ulation of the Sun in the out[...] In LV[...]

Melusine Lefay.

Then thereunder a circle has been drawn, with the same symbols as those engraved in the inner side of the ring under the stone.

Both men are silent. Jason notices all kinds of questions fighting for priority in his head. Variations on *'What is the purpose of this ring, who was the owner, what do the symbols mean,'* ranging into *'would the former owner be still alive?'* and even more questions that he is unable to formulate.

"Research it on the internet," William says.

"I did not bring my tablet," Jason answers. "I visited the sports school before I came to you. What keywords would you use, to find answers?"

"Look at YHVH, astrological symbols, and research on the name of Melusine Lefay, for a start. Dependent on the outcome, you need to dig deeper."

Jason thanks William for the help and quickly drives home. He feels frustrated that he did not take his tablet with him. "Normally I always carry it around with me," he grumbles to himself.

Back home he throws his jacket on the couch and grabs his computer. He opens it and waits impatiently until the device is ready to search. Tiger obviously wants attention; he arches his little back, hugs Jason's legs and meows. He pushes his head against Jason's hand. "No time, Tiger," Jason pushes him aside. Quick, the answers...

YHVH…Yes, the pictures pop up. William was right. Those are the letters surrounding the stone at the four corners of the square. Then he searches for 'astrological symbols' and again finds hits; pages full of strange hieroglyphs. Under the pictures are the words: "Sun, Moon, Mars, Mercury…He looks at the ring. Yes, they resemble the tokens under the stone. Virgo, Leo, Cancer, Scorpio, those are tokens in the outer edge. Next to the pictures is written 'planets and stars.' Clear… hmmm.

Another query … 'Melusine Lefay' this time. The first link brings him to a poem written by an old alchemist. Archaic language that feels weird and mysterious. He tries to understand the text, but for some reason it doesn't take:

> *Melusine, the Alchemical Siren:*
> *I am your Fluid Self, the Tincture of Transformation.*
> *I baptize you and purify your inner nature: from Nigero to Albedo.*
> *Thus I reveal to you the Spirit of Fluid Light,*
> *The Glory of the World.*

Hmmm, a riddle. Let's look further if there are any other hits on these words. Nothing special...wait a minute, it can also be a person. Someone has made a Facebook page with that name. But the content is protected. The only thing he can do is leave a message.

Thoughtful Jason walks towards the kitchen. Will he take the plunge and send a message to that person? Pondering about this possibility he makes himself a cup of coffee. Then he hears it again. What is that buzzing sound? He searches the entire kitchen and cannot find a cause.

He feels a strange and tickling feeling, as if ants are walking under his skin. Especially his forehead tingles and itches. Then he feels a boost of energy rising through his spine, upward, zigzagging, like a huge electrical pulse. The shocking feeling returns and he can no longer control his movements. His heart races, his hands burn, alarm! He breathes deeply and fast; Jason swallows his heart. The heat in his body rises and suddenly the light changes. What is this? For some reason everything looks differently. The colors intensify and everything appears to be suffused by a golden surrealistic light. He feels afire and the pulsations only increase in intensity, panic!

He walks to his favorite chair at the window and tries to calm himself. When he looks out of the window everything appears to be a part of an outlandish movie – the colors are too bright, the light too unnatural, the world looks disturbingly strange.

In a desperate attempt to distract himself, Jason grabs the remote control lying next to the chair on the floor. He pushes a button and falls in the middle of a discussion program.

The sound is quicker than the images. After some white noise the words sound, "You are talking about synchronicity. Can you explain what the meaning is of that word?" the interviewer asks.

Then the image follows. In a homey looking background a man and a woman are sitting on a leather couch. The space is lit by cobalt blue panels, a purple floor; the matching seats reflect these colors softly in their shining surface. In front of the couch is a picture of a circular disk, divided into twelve parts.

The scenery clearly forms the background of a spiritual show. Behind the couch where the hosts are seated is another panel and to Jason's dismay it shows an eye in a triangle, with the meaningful words underneath: For Your Eye Only. 'For your eye … that ought to be plural!' Jason thinks heavily irritated.

The interviewing woman starts her explanation, "Synchronicity is the appearance of meaningful coincidences. When synchronicity happens, the boundaries between the inner worlds and the outer world are gone. It is like a dream that suddenly becomes reality.[i]

"When you experience it, you are touched deep in your heart. It is as if a gateway opens between your daily life and the events of higher dimensions taking place outside of time. At that moment you become conscious of the fact that the world you take for real is in fact a dream. For some reason the all-encompassing reality of the universe penetrates your life and you get the strong feeling that you awaken in a lucid dream: that is the type of dream wherein you suddenly realize that you are dreaming."

'Strange,' Jason thinks and realizes at that very moment that the throbbing, the panic and the movements have gone. Even the colors have returned back to normal. Now he looks at the symbol that is engraved into the stone of the ring. It is the same symbol as the panel above the couch. 'For your Eye Only' and the Eye of the Winged Human Being appear at the same point in time in a television show about synchronicity. That cannot be a coincidence, can it? "Bullshit: New-Age nonsense," he takes the remote control and switches it to football.

*****

Bzzzzzzz, bzzzzzz, bzzzzz. Restless, he turns around in his sleep.

"Jason, Jaaason, Jaaasooon." It echoes in his dream. Giggling voices of girls. Jason is surrounded by a green color. He walks in a meadow with blooming flowers.

"Jason, Jaaason, Jaaaasoooon." He hears it clearly. Or is it the sound of a rippling creek? He walks towards it and sees a woman in gorgeous cloths. She wears a crown of flowers on her head and she is dressed in a white transparent gown. He can clearly see the form of her breasts through the fabric. Her feet are dangling in the water. When he looks at the water he sees waterlilies floating on the surface. The woman does not look at him, and the image changes into black-and-white.

"Jason, Jaaason, Jaaasoooon." Now the sounds come from a different direction, from the woods. He turns around and walks in the direction of the sound. He climbs over the wet rocks and walks to a black stone, polished so brightly that it mirrors the environment. Suddenly an image appears in the stone, the image of a red-haired woman. She seems to be sleeping. While he walks into her direction to figure out what is happening, he steps on a twig that breaks in two with a snapping sound. On that sound the image of the woman disappears in the stone.

"Jason, Jaaason, Jaaasooon." Apparently he fell again into a dreamless sleep. At the calling of his name he discovers that he now is in a meadow amidst of poppies and anemones. When he opens his eyes he looks straight into the blue eyes of a blonde woman. She is so close by that he feels her warmth and her lips almost touch his. At the moment he is about to kiss and embrace her, she disappears into thin air.

"Jason, Jaaason, Jaaasooon." The scene changes, and now a woman dressed in black walks towards him through a rose hedge, but as suddenly as she appeared, she vanishes into the shadows.

"Jason, Jaaason, Jaaasooon." A next seduction, as intangible as the prior ones. He feels how he reacts with burning passion, when a woman with curly hair, dressed in a nightgown walks by. Can he touch her legs while she passes him? He grabs into thin air.

"Jason, Jaaason, Jaaasooon," followed by the sound of rushing water. He walks into the river and feels the cold water surrounding him, the muddy ground under his feet and he follows a naked red-haired woman, who is standing in the water up to her waistline. In a moonlit scene she walks away from him with outstretched arms. The moon reflects in the water and suddenly she disappears in the waters.

"Jason, Jaaason, Jaaasooon," from a high rock the next woman calls him. She is seated in a waterfall—her feet dangling in the rushing water. Her wavy hair hangs around her shoulders like a curtain. She stretches her hand towards Jason, but the current is too strong, the waters wash him away.

"Jason, Jaaason, Jaaasooon." In a huge wave appears a face. The waves change into curly hairs, breasts gleaming in the water and when he looks at her legs ... she does not have legs but a fishtail! And as quickly as she emerges, she dissolves into the waves.

"Jason, Jaaason, Jaaasooon." From all sides the women come out of the water. They lure him, tempt him with their dancing hips and moving breasts. "Follow us, come with us," they caress him, look at him, take his hands, pull at his arms and draw him under water. He hears the rushing water, the splashing sound of the waves ... and the giggling.

One by one the faces appear, he feels their caressing hands, a slender lingering hand with sharp nails scratches him and leaves a trail of five grazes on his chest as a mark. He floats in the water, deeper and deeper, chasing the muses. Together with the girls he swims into a whirlpool and is dragged down deeper and deeper.

The water takes him; he feels the pull of the current. At the bottom of the whirlpool he sees the contours of a building looming up. When he comes closer he discovers, deep under the surface of the water, a drowned city.

Amazed, he studies the classical ornaments, the big tiles, and the huge pillars. Massive stone statues partially overgrown by seaweed. The girls show him the way and he swims behind them as if he belongs to a shoal of fishes, moving rhythmically to and fro as one organism. Deep beneath the surface of the water he discovers a structure that reminds him of a staircase, overgrown by water plants. The girls take him to a temple complex. Then they disappear into the waves and he rattles the rusty knocker of a door, in an attempt to get into the building.

The noise of a gong resonates through the water. The sound ripples like the waves. "Jason, Jaaason, Jaaasooon, what is the key that opens all doors?" Bewildered he looks around. 'Key? What key? Air! Where am I?'

He moves his arms wild around him and wakes up, bathing in sweat. He turns on the light and walks to the bathroom to drink a glass of water and recover from the intensive dream. He hears the sound of the rushing water from the tap. When he looks into the mirror of the bathroom, he turns deadly pale and stares to his mirror image. There, on his chest, he clearly sees the trace of those five long nails, scraped in his skin.

He looks at the clock — half past six. He might as well get up right away. Thoughtfully, he touches the scratches. It is too early to think about it now. He steps under the shower and dresses. Then he heads downstairs, to finish his early morning ritual. He checks his diary to see what jobs need to be done today. When he opens his tablet he faces the page that he visited last night: the Facebook page of Melusine Lefay. Impulsively, he types a message:

"I have bought a ring on the flea market. It came with an accompanying note with your name on it. Do you want to know more? Kind regards, Jason."

Then he checks his diary and realizes that his work takes him to the city of Groningen. A company will open its doors. They want a nice article in a glossy magazine, wherein all the benefits of their medical instruments are praised. He takes his breakfast into his car because he has to rush, his briefcase under his arm. While he is still busy pulling on his coat, the telephone rings for the first conversation of the day. The working week has started.

*****

My morning starts as usual, having breakfast seated on my sofa at the window. Next to me sits my laptop on a beautiful wooden side table. At my left side the indoor fountain burbles encouraging. At my right side are burning candles for people that need my help. I always find it a pleasure to watch and listen to the rushing waters, especially now when the lotuses are opening.

First of all I check my email to see whether I have received messages that need an urgent answer. I read the list of names, make notes and formulate answers to different people. I switch on my television screen to watch the news and think whether there are items that need to be addressed at my blog. Then I visit Facebook, and read the messages of my friends. I find a message of an unknown sender in my inbox. *Probably a loner, searching for a wife.* I click on the message and read:

"I have bought a ring on the flea market. It came with an accompanying note with your name on it. Do you want to know more? Kind regards, Jason."

I raise my eyebrows, and frown my forehead. Ring? Flea market? My name? What a strange message! I think deeply, my hand touches my mouth and thoughtfully I bring my forefinger to my lips. I concentrate and search my memory. In my mind I go back in time, to London where I lost my ritual ring years ago. That is impossible! That is too long ago and on top of that it was in a foreign country. But nevertheless… it is a charged ring, and those objects have a life of their own. In the light of the work that we have done recently on the project, it is to be expected that highly unlikely coincidences will happen. The message is intriguing. I decide to send a one-liner to figure out what this is all about.

"Ring? Note? I am curious, tell me more!!"

Jason hears a bleep coming from his tablet, a sign that he received a new message. He decides to make a short break to refuel and check his message box. A text message of William who writes him that the strange signs indeed are astrological symbols, a voicemail from Joan who tells him that she will come to collect a suitcase with cloths. She has decided that she needs at minimum a month to think things through. She has booked a holiday with her sister to think about her future and to figure out whether this journey will be together with him or not.

"I am thirty-three years old, my biological clock is ticking. I cannot wait endlessly until you are ready, Jason."

He is pissed off. He had hoped that she would come back when her anger was over. He can do without domestic problems at this moment in life! This is exactly the type of stress that he does not need right now. It means that he needs to think how to rearrange his household, now that he is alone all of a sudden. Then, the message of Melusine arrives. He reacts immediately. He describes the ring, the Hebrew letters, the six rays, the wings, the astrological tokens and the note.

I rub my eyes in disbelief when I read his answer. *That is my ritual ring indeed! Apparently the ring has chosen this man. That means that he has a task to do in the Great Work. I need to see him and speak to him. Let me find out whom I am dealing with.* Quickly my fingers hit the keyboard:

"You describe a ring that resembles the one that I have lost years ago. I would really want to see it. Is that possible?"

After the exchange of several messages, Melusine and Jason make an appointment to meet each other at a wayside restaurant along the highway. Jason thinks that he then has solved at least one problem: how to get a hot meal today. He will be on his way back home by then and does not even have to make a detour.

*****

The alarm of my telephone goes off and wakes me up from my deep concentration. I look at the clock and see that it is time to go to my appointment. Wonderful to leave the office after a day of working at the computer; it can be extremely tough without seeing anyone. *I have got quite a job done today. After meeting the guy that found my ring this evening, I can easily be back in time for the astral work that I have planned with my colleagues. That will be interesting, because I might be able to fill them in on the latest important information of this meeting.* I check my make-up. I have no clue what kind of person I will be meeting, so I decide to dress neutral and in business style. I don't want to scare him off and make him turn around immediately.

I take my make-up case and enter into the bathroom. The black mascara encircles my green-blue eyes. I comb my long black hair, spray it with hairspray to add more volume and keep it in place. Carefully, I paint my lips. Today I chose sea green cloths. They fit in with the weather and the season. Then I put my long coat and my head on, and I am ready for the meeting. I put my hand gloves on and at a last check in the mirror of the hall I push an obstinate curl back in place. Then I take my car keys and hit the road.

*****

The journey goes through heavy traffic and the mist does not make the drive easy. *Luckily the traffic is still moving,* Jason thinks while he observes the traffic that moves both at his left and his right side. There is the junction. A turn of the steering wheel, the last curve and then he arrives at the parking facility of the restaurant. It is extremely busy. The venue is adorned with early Christmas garlands, Christmas balls and on the tables are burning tea lights. *How to recognize this lady?* He decides to choose a seat at the entrance so that he can watch the door.

When Melusine enters the restaurant, Jason knows almost instinctively that this is his date. With her tall, slender figure, her remarkable eyes, her erected collar, Melusine is an intriguing appearance. Jason tries to guess her age, but gives up. The only thing he knows is that she is no youngster. Melusine takes off her gloves, shakes his hand, puts down her purse and takes off her long coat. They sit down and introduce themselves.

"So you have found my ring?" I prefer the direct approach, in such cases. I do not like small talk but come straight to the point.
Jason takes the box from his jacket and puts it in the middle of the table.
"Oh how wonderful, the original bone box is still with it," I say enthusiastically. "It is completely intact. May I?" I look at him studiously to see whether I am allowed to open the box. My hands caress the lit and the lock. I look at the box from every angle. Then

I unlock it. "The velvet inside has become pale through the years," I remark. The only purple that has kept its full color is the base of the double bottom.

And there is my ring! How wonderful to see it again after all these years! I am curious about the story of its whereabouts after it disappeared miraculously from my life. I look at the Hebrew letters. I admire the star sapphire, wherein clearly the triangle with the eye is still visible. "Yes that has been my ring indeed," I say to Jason. "How did you find it?"

Jason tells me the entire story of his journey through the mists and about the search on Waterloo Square. He tells me about the extraordinary attraction that this ring had on him, so much that he impulsively decided to buy it.

I look him in the eyes and measure the depths. He is a nice young man to see. He will be about 35 years of age. "A young dog," I think smiling. Reddish hair in a short haircut, slightly balding. He wears a stubbly beard like is fashionable among his peers. He has greyish eyes and a sporty appearance.

Then I look into his soul and notice that in his deep core, a change process is in full motion. I feel with my extra senses that he is at the beginning of an inner adventure, where he will need my help desperately. I notice his characteristics. He has the typical expression in his eyes, the subtlety in his mimics and gestures that are characteristic of the Old Ones, but he hasn't woken up yet. I realize that he is probably called by the ring and can be utterly confused by the new experiences that he needs to address. From my expertise I know how sweeping this can be and the amount of panic and confusion it can cause. It is so incredibly important that someone going through that process receives the right type of help. But in our materialistic culture, there are so few people that can guide a person through these changes. Not to mention to guide them through without causing harm to the psyche. Nowadays people need to go through the transformation process without the help of experienced Members of the Family and chances are big that someone gets lost. I need to think and feel how I can approach him in such a way that he opens himself to guidance, to help him with his awakening process.

"You have bought the Lapis Sancti Magi," I say. "That is a very special ring; it is worn within a small unknown order of spiritually trained people. I have lost this ring years ago and for me it is a small miracle that it returns into my life in this way. My question is why you found it. Are you by any means interested in transpersonal development; are you a seeker for the meaning of life?"

"I have never been occupied by transpersonal development," Jason answers. "I do not understand what it is exactly and what people get out of it," he answers.

"For some people it is inevitable," I answer, "Sometimes things happen in life that confront you with the fact that there is an invisible dimension to reality. Not a faith, but as a faix a complit, an undeniable experience. When you start to investigate these events, you find out that these transpersonal experiences have been studied and that there is a philosophical and theoretical model that acknowledges their reality, shapes them and structures them."

Now the journalist in Jason awakens slowly and interested he bends forward. "What type of experiences are you talking about?" he asks, while the hairs on his arms rise.

"In some people a layer of consciousness awakens, that causes the Other Reality to penetrate into their normal waking consciousness. Among them are very famous people that changed their professional views because of these experiences. Some examples are Emanuel Swedenborg, Isaac Newton and Carl Gustav Jung.

"Slowly you start to understand that your entire concept of spirituality is built upon a childish worldview. That there is an adult vision on the deeper layers of reality. When you chose to follow this road of development, it triggers peak experiences, existential ecstasy and a completely different outlook on the cause of events. Jason, I have a serious question for you. Do you have unnatural experiences since you are in possession of this ring?"

Jason sighs. Does he need to tell this completely unknown woman about his panic attacks? About his bewildering dreams, of the television show about synchronicity, the scratches on his chest caused by a mermaid in his dreams?

I see the different facial expressions changing on Jason's face and I am able to see some of the Thoughtforms behind them. He most certainly has supernatural experiences, but he does not want to talk about them. I see how one of the Muses marks him in his dream. No, about that experience he will not talk at this point in time. The going needs to get tougher will he start to talk about that, now he tries to deny his experiences with full effort.

"When you are interested in finding out more about the ring and want to visit our training group, I invite you to pass by. It happens regularly that a visitor comes with questions about what we are and what we are doing. The coffee is always ready for those who are sincerely interested, and want to have a taste about the whereabouts of the group." I take a business card from my handbag and slide it towards him over the table. "You can give me a call when you get worried about your supernatural experiences. When an object has been used in the way that this ring was used, it will inevitably cause changes in your life. When you decide that you no longer want to possess this ring, I kindly ask you to contact me because maybe I want to buy it back from you."

The alarm on my telephone reminds me of the fact that I need to say goodbye now, because I have an appointment with the 'Others' tonight. I hold my findings of this evening for very important and I think it is essential to inform them right away about the reappearance of my lost magical ring. I say goodbye to Jason and emphasize to contact me when necessary. He answers that he will consider visiting the group. We shake hands; I step in my car and drive home.

*****

My house is pitch black when I arrive. I switch on the lights and make myself a cup of coffee. I need to stay awake and alert for a while. Then I start to change my clothing and ignite the candles of my meditation room. I feel how the supple long fabric of my ritual robe dances around my legs and I experience deep wondrous feelings slowly awakening inside of me. I turn on some ritual music and watch the awakening of my ritual space, while I am preparing myself.

Great Kabbalistic Cross

Then I approach the altar. I connect myself with the spiritual dimensions by means of the Great Kabbalistic Cross. I raise my right arm towards the ceiling and in my mind I contact the Higher Worlds.

I vibrate: "Ateh[2]." Then I bring down my left hand, point towards the Earth and resonate "Malkuth[3]," I feel a lightning flash of energy rushing through my arms and spine and note clearly how the electrical energy awakens in my body.

I raise my arms; palms turned outwards at both sides of my head, and vibrate: "Ve-Chokmah[4], Ve-Binah[5]." I feel my third eye opening and my ability to contact the deeper psychic levels increases.

I notice how the contact with the Inner Planes intensifies, how a higher power rushes through my body, like a waterfall of pleasure entering my head from above, activating the inner sight of my

---

[2] To Thou
[3] The Kingdom
[4] Wisdom
[5] Understanding

third eye. At that moment my environment starts to radiate with a supernatural light; this is the effect the awakening of the 'Star Chamber of Isis' has on me.

I bring my hands together at my throat and vibrate: "Da'ath[6]." The sound of the vibration of the word opens the 'Interior Star' in my throat; I open my heart to devotion. My concentration on the work and the experiences of my inner worlds deepen. In my head a channel opens, accessing higher wisdom and I widen the contact lines to the Wisdom of the Stars. My extra senses stretch out like they are big antennae receiving the knowledge from the cosmos.

Then I stretch my hand outwards on throat level again and intonate a second time, "Da'ath," and my left hand points towards the earth again, and I resonate, "Malkuth," the gesture by which I confirm that I offer the higher wisdom that I receive to serve the earth.

Now I stretch out my arms as wide as possible over the horizon, I look at my right hand and vibrate towards the palm of my hand, "Ve –Geburah."[7] I switch my attention to my left hand and vibrate: "Ve-Gedulah."[8] I clearly feel how the Sphere of Sensation expands and I become capable of sensing my far environment, receiving impressions and sensations over distances. I slowly turn into a big sensible receiver of the ales and needs of the world.

---

[6] Knowledge
[7] Severity
[8] Mercy

I bring my hands together before my heart and visualize a flaming light in my heart and vibrate: "Tiphareth."[9] At that moment the 'Interior Star of the Sun' becomes alive in my heart and starts to radiate and beat. The beating and pulsating feelings of love and compassion go out to my environment to everyone I am conscious of, which can use this radiating warmth.

My right hand stays at the same place, now my left hand points downwards and I vibrate: "Malkuth." With this gesture the heart-energy streams into the earth and I make it available for those who need it.

Then I bring down both arms, the palms of my hands point outwards at the level of my hips. I vibrate, "Ve-Hod[10], Ve-Netzach,"[11] I feel how these powers come alive in me. In my imagination my legs change into two huge pillars giving me power and support, thus supplying me with unwavering power matching me up against everything.

Now I fold my hands together at my genital center, the Interior Star of the Moon starts throbbing, a wave of vitality and life force flows through my body. Also these forces I offer to the earth, I vibrate: "Yesod."[12] At that moment I feel how my Sphere of

---

[9] Beauty
[10] Glorious Radiation
[11] Power to Overcome
[12] The Mystery

Sensation grows. It makes me think of the scene in Alice in Wonderland when Alice swallows the pill to grow. My feet are like roots, connected to the deepest core of the earth and my spine changes into the World-axis, my hair change into a direct wiring connecting me with the stars.

"Yesod—Malkuth." Also the life giving forces of miracles and marveling I offer to the Earth.

Then I bring my right hand up again, above my head and vibrate: "Ateh, Malkuth." I stretch my arms horizontally. "Ve-Geburah, Ve-Gedulah," and bring them together in my heart, "Le Olam, Amen."

Now I am connected to the earth and at the same time tuned into the Inner Levels. I empower my meditation by the familiar formulas to sink deeper and deeper into a meditative trance.

> *Now do I descend into the Inner Seas,*
> *That move as ebb and flood inside my soul.*
> *Let me descend the stairway of time,*
> *Back into the Eternal Time,*
>
> *Where the Gods are walking the Earth,*
> *And everything is exactly as it should be.*

The spiral staircase reappears, just like a few days ago. I pick up the torch and start the long descent. The familiar echoing sound of my footsteps on the stones, deeper and deeper downstairs, until I am back in front of the gate. I knock and recite the access spell:

> *I ask access to the Holy City,*
> *Build on an island in the Cosmic Ocean:*
> *Open yourself to me, Temple of Lights,*
> *Sculptured from Lapis Lazuli stone,*
> *Build for the rites of Magicians and Priests,*
> *House for the Incantations of Heaven and Earth,*
> *Where no evil can permeate;*
> *It is encircled and protected by the Web of Light.*

Leo, the Guardian reappears and brings me to the other shore. I see the rocky island looming up. I feel the wind blowing through my robes, my hair whirl around my head. In the distance I see the fire baskets burning that mark the entrance of the temple.

Just a few moments, and then I set foot on the ancient continent. I climb the stairs and take the iron knocker in my hand. I knock at the door that gives access to the temple. From behind the door I hear a voice, "What is the key that opens all doors?"
Self-assured, I answer, "The name of the Key of Keys is Devotion."

The double doors swing open and I clearly hear the sound of the crispy wood, the grinding hinges. I change cloths as usual and enter into the great hall. The others have also arrived. They bow.

"Welcome High priestess, Lady of the Lake." I take my seat at the great throne in the North between the Pillars of Equilibrium. I make a connection with the Warrior-Monk, who is seated directly opposite of me. I look him in the eyes and I feel how the forces zigzag between us. At my left and my right side, the Lady of the Planetary Deva and the Walker-between-the-Worlds make a similar connection. Then I speak in the mind to my colleagues:

"The Lapis Sancti Magi has reappeared," I say. "It has reconnected with my by the hands of a young man, whose name is Jason. He is one of the Old Family, but he is sleeping. The ring is busy waking him up, but due to his upbringing and education he is strictly trained in using his logical mind. On top of that he became a victim of our history during one of his former incarnations.
"I fear that this young man will be going through a touch period in his life when he does not get our help. It has been clear to us that the finder of this ring would turn out to be one of us, but this young man has almost no background in the Great Work in this life. When his memories start to surface, we will need to pay attention that he does not go over the top and ends in a psychosis. There is so little help around him that I am sincerely worried."

I catch the thoughts of the Warrior-Monk clearly. "So many of us choose not to wake up to the Inner Planes because of these old traumas that stigmatized their souls. This makes them cripple in their spiritual assignment. These old traumas cause the Western world to almost lose the connection between the spiritual 'Above' and the Earthly 'Below.'

"The world has gradually turned into a pool of sharks, instead of being a place where people incarnate to develop their life's mission or a place where it is enjoyable to linger for everyone."
I answer telepathically. "This man obviously has an extraordinary important task. By his efforts he can become the trailblazer for many who want to follow his steps and enable them to go through a similar experience. Let us offer him extra protection so that he is surrounded by helping forces and people who can guide him through the process."
The Lady of the Planetary Deva adds her thoughts to the wordless conversation, "The Earth is in need of this type of development. This man will initiate an expanding consciousness. It needs to be done, by this man or by someone else. Inevitably he will be tested. When the gates to the Otherworld open for him he needs to be trained. The first obstacle he needs to conquer is the Test of Earth, the ability to discriminate. Like the ancient Greek story of Eros and Psyche he will need to learn to divide between seeds and ashes, truth and illusions. I give him a gift, the 'Seed of the Tree of Life.' When he discovers the Kabbalistic Tree and starts to work with it, the channels for his development will open harmoniously, so that the snake-energy does not burn him."

The Walker-between-the-Worlds formulates his thoughts loud and clear, "Let us send him some guides, so that he will find his way more easily when the Gates between the Worlds open to him. I will guide him with insights and realizations and lead him by coincidences. In his dreams I will educate him and send the right people on his path. I will teach him how to receive inspiration and guidance from nature and from the people and animals that surround him."

We knot towards each other. Then I take the thurrible and purify the space. The Lady of the Planetary Deva sprinkles salt around, the Warrior Monk spreads his purifying fire and the Walker-between-the-Worlds create a waterway. On the altar there is still sleeping the human baby with a beating heart.

I take the torch that is hanging in a holder at the wall next to my seat. I light it from a star. The scintillating light spreads a radiating energy through the entire temple space.
I make the symbolic gestures to open the doors to the Spiritual Reality:

>*I open the Double Doors of the Star Temple*
>*And ignite the lighting beacon of the North.*

>*I ignite my torch from the fire of the Royal Star Fomalhaut*
>*And call upon the Winged Human Being:*
>*Come to us and take your seat*
>*At the Watchtower of Obsidian in the North.*
>*Illuminate the beacon*
>*and open the procession road to the House of Light*

Then the Lady of the Planetary Deva takes my torch. She ignites the fires on the altar and follows me in the invocation:

> *I open the Double Doors of the Star Temple*
> *And ignite the lighting beacon of the East.*
> *I ignite my torch from the fire of the Royal Star Aldabaran*
> *And call upon the Winged Bull:*

> *Lord of Form, you who are the manifesting power of the Earth,*
> *Of what is ordained by the Heavens,*
> *Take your place on the Watchtower of Turquoise;*
> *Open the Gates of Abundance of spring,*
> *Illuminate our procession road to the House of Light.*

She passes the torch on to the Warrior-Monk. He repeats the movements and ignites the third fire in the temple. With his deep resonating voice he fills the space:

> *I open the Double Doors of the Star Cathedral*
> *And ignite the lighting beacon of the South.*
> *I ignite my torch from the fire of the Royal Star Regulus*
> *And call upon the Winged Lion:*

> *Lord of Flames, illuminate us with the highest integrity,*
> *Open our hearts for this light and come to us.*
> *Take your place on the Watchtower of Amber,*
> *Illuminate the beacon of summer*

And open the procession road to the House of Light.

Then the torch is passed on to the Walker-between-the-Worlds. His fires emblaze the entire temple with a scintillating light:

I open the Double Doors of the Star Cathedral
And ignite the lighting beacon of the West.
I ignite my torch from the fire of the Royal Star Antares
And call upon the Eagle, the Lord of Mind,
Who transmits the messages between Gods and humanity.

Holy Phoenix who hatches the egg of the renewing tradition,
Come to us and take your place at the Watchtower of Sapphire.
Illuminate the beacon of autumn
And open the procession road to the House of Light.

In a flash, four winged beings appear around the altar, embedded in a bluish light. The flames give away and give access to a surrealistic landscape. The four of us surround the altar and a whirlwind of forces moves like a blue-flaming vortex around the altar. It is an amazing sight.

Together, we step with our torches towards the central altar. We raise our torches in such a way that the flames become one above the altar. Then we speak simultaneously:

We ask access to the Lands of Joy.
We call upon the King called Total Vision.
Dressed in the Black Mantle of the night:

Guardian of the Sacred Mountain,
Illuminate our temple with your two eyes,
Take your seat upon the days and show us the way.

A triangle with one eye appears above the altar, surrounded by a vortex of blue flames. At both sides of my seat in the North, shapes start to appear in the flames. They draw together in two images: the image of the Sun appears at my left side and the image of the Moon to my right.

Then I encircle the temple. I fill the thurrible with storax incense and envelop the entire temple in thick smoke. Delighting in the exquisite smell, I breathe in the scented air. When I am done I place the thurrible next to the clay baby at the main altar. We now sit down and look with full intention to what happens. From my robe I take my writing pad to make notes in automatic writing.

The heart of the baby now starts to pulsate. Rays of light shoot from its heart. I watch closely to what happens and I try to note down as many details as possible.

"A white weapon shield with a lance with three points on it. It looks a bit like the French Lilly, but is curlier. Red and white, a building in Italian style, made of big yellow building blocks, a curved apex."

I don't see any more details and then the vision fades. We take our torches, raise them and kneel down on one knee in front of the altar. With our other hand we make a fist and bring it to our chest. Then we close down the ritual.

We look at each other one last time and turn around, to go back to our daily lives. Back to the great hall, through the double doors, over the staircase of time, back into the meditation room.

When I am fully back in my physical body I notice how cold it has become. The candle on the altar is almost burned down. This must have taken hours. I pinch out the candles and leave the meditation room. In my office I turn on the light and study the notes that I have made during the ritual. I record everything as detailed as possible and email my conclusions to my three colleagues who will probably be doing the same thing from their houses. I am excited to learn what information they have received from the Contact. This can turn out to become an extraordinary adventure!

THE SEARCH FOR DRY LAND

3

THE SEARCH FOR DRY LAND

The alarm goes off. It is the typical grey Monday morning that makes you want to hide under your blankets instead of leaving your bed. Jason sighs. He could sleep for hours. In spite of being rested after the weekend, he feels completely exhausted. All his muscles ache and he feels a strong resistance to start the day. He is fully dredged by the roller coaster of emotions, by the long working days without rest and the pressure to have everything finished yesterday. In the coming weeks taking a break from work will not be an option, so he has to bite it, continue on willpower and try to survive the stress.

Tiger isn't aware of Jason's issues. As soon as Jason has opened his eyes he looks into two exited happy kitty eyes. Tiger is looking forward to the day and rushes down the stairs in front of Jason, longing for his breakfast.

Jason works his way through his morning ritual and while he makes the last moves to leave for work, the telephone rings. On the display he sees that his colleague is trying to reach him. 'Harry is extremely early today,' Jason thinks while he picks up the phone. He listens to the quick voice of Harry.

"Hey chap, listen: I just now opened my email. Guess what? We have been invited to that congress about modernizations in healthcare! I am allowed to send a reporter to the event, something for you?"

Jason has to switch. So much enthusiasm is difficult to process for his depressed mind. "What do you mean?" he asks.

"The congress about new pharmaceutical treatment methods for illnesses in Florence! That could be the start of a larger series of articles for Caduceus Magazine!"

Finally Jason realizes what Harry means. They have been informed about the upcoming congress a while ago, and Jason has already prepared himself and red some literature. "Ghee that came quicker than expected," he mumbles.

"This can produce a lot of extra work. It would be a very interesting development for our company to specialize in medical journalism. There is an awful lot of money to be made in that industry," Harry continues enthusiastically. "In Florence we could start to build on an interesting network with established professionals in that branch to develop our expertise. There is a series of similar congresses in the planning; all of them will give us international exposure. In other words, the next step to expand our network is Florence. Jason, now that your girlfriend has run away, you can probably use some distraction? How do you feel about buying a ticket to Florence to look around and report the congress?"

Jason raises his eyebrows, his breath stops for a moment and all kinds of blocking thoughts shoot like arrows through his head, for a moment he is confused. He holds his breath because of the unexpected change of plans in the early morning. Then he takes a deep breath and says, "Yessss...When?"

Harry and Jason read through the email and make a list of the things that are important for the project. Then they research on the Internet and put together a list of names of people and clinics that could make an interesting start. Jason asks his neighbor whether she is able to feed Tiger the next coming days. He books a plane ticket and a hotel. Everything goes smoothly and he finds a flight that will leave at 6 pm to Italy. "Florence, here I come," he says to his mirror image and starts to pack his suitcase.

A few hours later he hovers above the city and looks down from the plane window at the breath-taking view of Florence at sunset. A golden horizon illuminates the houses and reflects in the waters of the river. He sees the dome of the Santa Maria del Fiore and the Ponte Vecchio. After he passes through customs, he takes a cap that drives him along impressive buildings to his hotel room. 'Now life is good to me again,' Jason thinks and relaxes.

He looks around in the hall of the great hotel. His eyes glide along the details of the Renaissance building. He admires the forms, the lights and colors, the statues carved from stone. In awe he observes the pillars that support the great hall and the arched ceiling. He stares intensively to the ceiling from where an extraordinary light enters the hall through huge glass stained windows. He admires the wooden roses framing the windows. The marble floor is inlayed in a complex mosaic pattern. His hands touch the beautifully made carved banisters alongside of the stairs. Jason loves everything that is real, that shows craftsmanship and love for the profession. He sighs and the tension falls from his shoulders. Wonderful when you are able to express the love for your profession in paintwork and marble.

"I wished I could be a craftsman in my profession of journalism," he thinks passionate. "All those prefabricated articles and ordered opinions have made my profession a propaganda monster. I have been drifting off from my basic ethical foundations, like researching for truth and informing the public. Instead I have become a common copywriter.

"When I think about this project, it is a really nice surprise. I hope this will give me the opportunity to make a truly spicy report. That is exactly what I need right now." He feels much better than when he left home, eagerly looking forward to the events of the coming days.

The next day he is up early because he wants to visit some tourist attractions before the congress starts. He has made an appointment with Angelo Mercurio, an Italian tour guide. Angelo will show him the way into the world of the Florentine Renaissance and guide him through one of the most famous buildings. The guide is waiting for him with a cardboard sign, his name written on it in the hotel lobby. Enthusiastically, he shakes Jason's hand.

"Buongiorno signore Adams, did you have a good journey?" With a warm Italian handshake, he greets Jason and starts a conversation in an Italian version of the English language. He proposes to make a detour through ancient Florence while visiting some interesting buildings. With a proud upright chest and a macho walk, Angelo leads Jason through the old city along the interesting places.

"At your left side is the birth house of Dante Alighieri. He was a very famous poet, who left us an important work, 'La Divina Comedia.' The story is about the love Dante had for the girl, Beatrice. Beatrice died and Dante loved her so much that he wrote a long poem about his quest. He heard the voice of the Beatrice and followed it through hell and purgatory, until he was able to reunite with her and embrace her in paradise."

They walk along the small houses and Angelo tells Jason that Beatrice was buried in a church in Florence. "Many young women go to her grave and leave notes to ask Beatrice for help and assistance in complicated love matters."

Angelo and Jason visit the famous buildings of Florence including the museum where fantastic paintings are exposed to the public. Then Angelo explains the influence of the Renaissance on Florence and why it was such an extraordinary time.

"It was a cultural golden age. You need to realize that the Middle Ages were pretty barbaric and analphabetic. The churches had an iron grip on society. But the power of the churches was broken in a very special way. In the early Middle Ages, a group of Arabic sages landed on the southern costs of Spain and started to educate people. During the Middle Ages, Arabic texts were translated to Latin and copied. The Wisdom Texts spread all over educated Europe in the form of the Toledo Letters and were studied by the European elite.

"The Toledo Letters were extremely important because they spread an interconnected spiritual and philosophical system, connected to the Arab prophet Idris—the Arabic name for Hermes Trismegistus. These teachings were regard to be the 'Science of the Sacred,' and the Wisdom Texts spread among scientists, monks and noblemen. Via Spain it heavily influenced European art and science, and still underpins our modern western culture.

"After the Arabic texts, the Greek texts of Plato and of Hermes Trismegistus found their way into Europe. They were translated in Florence. The philosophy got a name: Hermeticism, after Hermes Trismegistus and its ideas sparked off the Renaissance.

"This was the start of a great cultural revival in all areas of life. Painters became inspired by the great Greek myths. Operas were written with Hermetic ideas in the background. You can see that in the works of art from that period in time. It was a rebirth of the values and the cultures of classical times. The paganistic ideas came to full blossom as never before. Hermeticism became a source of inspiration for the higher classes of society. Not only in Florence, but in many European courts the works of Hermes Trismegistus were studied, and Arabic Astrology, Magic and Alchemy were more or less secretly practiced."

"What makes Hermeticism so special?" Jason asks.

"Hermeticism came to Europe from Chaldea and Greece. The philosophy is based on a series of tractates, called the Corpus

Hermeticum. They summarize the spiritual worldview of ancient Egypt, Babylon, Persia and Greece. The books explain the sacred philosophy that underpins Alchemy, Astrology, Magic, Gnosticism and Platonism. The story tells that these Sacred Texts were written by a God named Hermes Trismegistus, the Three-Times-Great Hermes. Based on this ancient philosophy, a Platonic Academy was founded in Florence, where people could study these ancient mysteries. Come with me, we are very close to the library, where some of the Hermetic books of major importance are preserved." Angelo points towards the monument that is built in the typical Florentine style.

Directly behind the entrance, Jason and Angelo step into a courtyard. The open garden is surrounded by a row of pillars; they support an arched ceiling. In the middle of the garden are hedges, planted and cut in geometrical shapes. Small roofs made from red tiles create extra shade. Jason's footsteps echo on the stone pavement when they walk the long corridors. Together with Angelo, he climbs the imposing marble staircases. He admires the woodwork of the bannisters and the reliefs carved in the imposing ceilings. Wherever he looks, he sees craftsmanship of the highest quality. His hands caress the flower motives carved in the old wood at the sides of the stairs.

Then they arrive at a row of wooden bureaus placed in an endless corridor.

'This is a cathedral of knowledge." Stained glass windows show strange pictures: two sea goats decorate a symbolic gateway, two angels dancing around a crown. And then suddenly ... it starts again!

Jason starts sweating; his breathing becomes heavy and quick. He tries to hide from Angelo what is happening to him, and he fakes interest in his environment. He walks between the other visitors after his guide. His skin aches; it feels like ants are walking under his skin, especially under his forehead. And the heat! As a hot fever it rages upwards along his spine, like a fiery snake, zigzagging up and down his body. He sees lightning flashes, and feels panic rising. 'This is not okay, what is going on' … and then he hears the deep buzzing sound again.

A mosaic on the floor with pictures of animals, a long corridor with a bended ceiling adorned with wooden roses. Closets full with ancient books, bound in leather, exposed behind glass windows. He walks along the exposition of books. They are completely handmade. The pages are made of parchment and handwritten in a beautiful handwriting. He hears the voice of the guide. "11,000 Manuscripts, 2500 papyri," The figures dazzle through his head. He has lost his concentration … "a collection of 126,000 books about … " and he sees the symbols dancing around him. They appear to have come alive. Does he hear music? No that is impossible. It is as if he gets bigger, bigger than his body. Something echoes in his head 'remember, remember!'

Angelo points at a bust of a Renaissance philosopher: "Marsilio Ficino." Jason is sweating and meanwhile has only one thought: how to get outside as quickly as possible and get some fresh air! He invites Angelo to have a cup of cappuccino outside at the terrace. Away from the building and back in the rushing city they look for a place to sit down. Jason looks at his environment. He is still disorientated and confused.

He loosens his tie, but that doesn't make any difference. The entire light has changed. It is as if everything has become covered with a golden veil. When he looks around him he sees an unrealistic beauty. Everything glitters as if made from gold. The people resemble caricatures, marionettes, and pictures from a strip magazine.

Jason watches the clock and to his relief he notices that it is time to say goodbye to Antonio for today. He needs to prepare for the congress. But deep inside he can only think of getting some rest in his hotel room to find himself again. When he has recovered he will do some extra research on the Internet for names of scientists and take a cap to the congress building.

After the congress, Jason decides to walk back to the hotel instead of taking a taxi. He squeezes his hands into fists in the pockets of his trousers, while he walks alongside of the river. He thinks about the important issues of his life. *I don't have a place for children. I do not want to take on this type of responsibility.* In his thoughts he hears Joan's words: "Yes but I am your own wife? What do you mean by 'keeping your hands free?' When we belong together, we both give one hundred percent?"
While he overlooks the rushing water and watches the wild waves falling over the rocks, he thinks: *I don't want to commit myself in such a way. I want my eyes to wonder, to travel the world when*

my job offers me that opportunity. A relation is nice as long as it is fun. But I am fed up with the endless tensed silences. And I am finished with the discussions about the future. I have something important to do. I feel that deep inside. The only thing is that I don't know what exactly that important task is? Do I need to break off a relationship of five years over our disagreement on having children? What does that say about me? Does that mean that I am a lonely traveler relation wise? Joan's angry words resonate hard and painful. "I am not a disposable woman. I want to have a real connection with a man."

Jason has now arrived at the lobby of the hotel and takes the lift to his room. When he has entered, he falls on the bed, tired, so tired...

The sound of rushing water. Jason finds himself at the top of the dyke and watches how the river slowly rises. The power of the water is amazing. It splashes against the shores and huge waves fall over the edge of the dyke. The place where he is standing is slowly getting drowned. In the water faces appear. *Remember, remember!* But before he can recognize them, they have already disappeared. He sees waves with foamy heads rising in greyish water. His breath is high in his chest and his heart squeezes together. Still he cannot do anything else but look. His shoes are under water right now. And even more water splashes in waves over the dyke. Objects drift upon the surface: litter that has been thrown carelessly in the water, natural materials like big branches with leafs drift on the surface of the river. More dangerous than the litter is the pollution of the water, the toxic chemicals. The plastic bottles are the most innocent objects, because they are clearly visible and drift on the surface. Most treacherous and dangerous is the unseen pollution, the poison, the medication, the industrial pollution and agricultural poisons. They are the invisible threat making the water sickening.

Waves splash over the shores. They resemble wild animals, sea goats jumping out of the water and falling back into the current. The trees at both sides shake because of the violent forces of the waters. Jason observes them fascinated, *I hope the dykes don't break.*

The water rushes and on the sound of the water a voice is heard: "Jason, you will not find your answers by your head, let yourself be carried by your soul. The world has a soul and everything floats on the waves of a shared Deep Consciousness. Know that this United Consciousness takes shape and lives in all matter. This connected field of consciousness condensates and in this way the ensouled world comes into being, together with the living stars. There is nothing on this world that is not ensouled. Awaken yourself, yes, you!

You are a part of it; you are a God in a human body.[ii] Jason sees a typical Florentine building with a big arched gateway, a flat roof and small window coverings that prevent the daylight from entering into the building. The gate opens and he sees a company of men, dressed in red capes. They wear hats that resemble a fez. They are engaged in an intensive conversation.

The flow of water rushes further. The waves now resemble grey armies of jockeys riding horses. An alarming mass that hardly stays in between the borders, and splashes with a dangerous force against the shores. Again the voice echoes: "Search for the source of metamorphoses and transformations, seek for the secrets of the Ancient Ones, contact the Old Family! Realize that you are a being from Heaven and not from the Earth! Discover the Interior Rooms of your mind. Decorate them with the most beautiful furniture, with meaningful pictures, with the most splendid symbolical objects and with sacred regalia, because you are a divine being, clothed in human flesh."[iii]

The dangerous waters now uproot a tree. It slowly falls over, into the rushing waters and is carried off on the waves.
"Open the 'Book of Life' and practice the 'Work of the Sun,'" and then an Eye appears in a Triangle! From the eye shoot six rays in different directions. "For Your Eye Only," it echoes around him. Four Hebrew letters dance around the eye. Each of the letters changes into a being of fire. Meanwhile the entire land is flooded with water. Jason stands amidst of a dangerous whirling mass of water. The four fire beings turn around him and form a chain hanging vertically. YHVH, thus creating a huge pillar. Two lightning bolts hit and shoot in different directions, resembling two wings of light, illuminating the entire horizon and setting it ablaze.
Then the four fire beings drift apart. They appear before him, behind him, at his left and at his right side, huge, filling the horizon. They resemble watchtowers, beacons of light amidst of a whirling ocean in a deep dark night.

... And in a shock Jason sits upright and awakens from his dream. He is soaking wet from sweating. He switches on the light and in an impulse he walks to his computer and writes a message to Melusine:

"I think that the ring messes with my brain. Can I speak to you when I am back in the Netherlands?"

He quickly hits the send button to prevent himself from rethinking... and regrets it immediately.
What will that completely unknown woman think of me? What is the time? Four a.m.? Do I dare to return back to sleep? What if things get awkward again? He walks to the fridge of the hotel room and discovers a small bottle of whiskey. In one sip he drinks a portion of forgetfulness and falls in a deep dreamless sleep.

*****

I open my computer to download the emails. Some of them hold interesting questions of people that I know for a while. I answer some of them with one single sentence; others take more time to answer. While I study their names, the images of the people behind the question form in my head. One by one the energy lines open, that connect me to them. Interesting, Jason Adams has send me a message. What would he have to say? I pour myself a cup of coffee and take a seat. Then I open his message and start to read. My eyes penetrate deep into the reality behind the words. I read the thoughts and emotions behind the sentences, the questions that did not reach the paper... Fortunately Jason gets a little bit more open and asks for help. It is a short message, but those few words are enough for my sixth sense to tune into his psyche. I repeat the sentences as if they are mantras. I connect with the sounds of the words. They resonate in me and I feel the different emotions shining through. The words open me to his experiences and my heart reaches out to him, when I feel the panic behind the words, the heartbeat, the restlessness and the shock about what he is going through. *His inner world is opening. He resonates on the old history of the Family, but he completely lacks the background to understand what is happening to him*, I mumble inside.

I stare in my coffee and let the words go through me again. I concentrate on the images that appear at the black shining surface, I feel his raging energy, and I experience the flood wave in his soul, his unspoken panic and feel that he reaches out for something tangible to hold onto. I notice the fear to be drowned into an ethereal illogical reality. I read the emotions on an even deeper level and witness how he has contacted the Wisdom of the Tradition. I see rows of books appearing before my inner eye, probably an old library. I penetrate even deeper, tune into the images. An open book, leafs of parchment, a Latin text. Ouch, that is difficult. I need all my concentration to figure out what is happening to him. I let the impressions resonate in my body once again, like a video movie that you can play back to repeat a scene. I try to receive this impression very precise. By visiting the library Jason obviously has picked up a vibration that speeds up the process in him. Then I get hold of the feeling of the words:

"About the Power of the Words and Songs, to receive the Heavenly Gifts and about the Seven Steps leading to these Heavenly Fruits."[iv]

Hmmm, that sounds as if he contacted one of the ancient Kabbalists, or maybe even one of the old Magi. I ponder what the best approach would be for him and then I write an email to my colleagues abroad, to inform them about the developments. I suggest speeding up the process of the astral work that is planned ahead. We need to support Jason on the Inner Planes, by activating the pattern that has been used by the Tradition since Antiquity. I consider it to be of the utmost importance that he is able to calibrate on that matrix of harmony as quickly as possible. I want to prevent him from getting confused or unstable, from the danger that his inner awakening process needlessly changes into a psychic crisis. He will need all the help he can get to develop himself without problems. Luckily Dindrane, Michael and Eagle are online and they react quickly at my proposal. *Excellent, we can start right away; everyone is able to tune in this evening.* Now that we have talked things through, I start the preparations.

I change cloths and enter into the meditation room. With full concentration I perform the preparation rituals. It is a fixed series of physical, emotional, mental and visual gestures combined with mental states, that I have practiced for years. It enables me to access the deepest layers of the Inner Worlds. My body switches over to the sleep modus, but my mind stays fully awake and focused. I enter into the state of mind that is sometimes called lucid dream consciousness; I consciously create images on the Inner Planes and perform ritual activities with a secure precision. I know that my colleagues preparing with the same precision each from their own meditation rooms: we will be able meet and communicate in the Inner Temple on the Astral level within a few minutes. In this way we will activate the Matrix for Jason together, without the necessity to meet each other physically.

I walk down the spiral staircase; I am on my way to the Temple of Lights. When I have given the Guardian the correct passwords I enter into the ritual room. I am the first one to arrive this time. After having taken my seat in the North, I start to build images around me with full concentration. I visualize double doors in the four walls of an imaginary room. In the center of the space, the altar with the clay baby is still present. Its heart beats powerful and regular. Then I see a movement in the astral atmosphere in the South and I witness the manifestation of the Warrior-Monk. I greet him. We look each other deep in the eyes and the energy is building. Together we raise the palms of our hands and the room becomes electrically charged. I see how at my left and right side the shapes of the Lady of the Planetary Deva and the Walker-Between-the-Worlds crystallize. I feel a flame of love and warmth rushing through me, filling the atmosphere. I contact the stellar constellations around the North Pole and from them I channel a pulsating energy into the temple space.
The Warrior-Monk catches these energies and adds his vital force to them. He sends the current of mixed energies towards the Walker-Between-the-Worlds, who adds his powerful images to the mixture. He charges them with a wave of intuitive knowing. Then

the current crosses over to the Lady of the Planetary Deva, who pours down the energies into malls, so that they can be applied to achieve concrete goals. She connects everything to the heart of the clay baby. When the energies flow around powerfully and a large amount of astral substance is hovering above the altar, we proceed with the next phase of the work. We contact the Lighthouses in the four Cardinal Directions. Now the form has become solid enough to move on to the next phase. I turn around and open the Double Doors of the North. I call up the Mists of Time and contact the Winged Human Being:

> *I call across the Oceans of Time,*
> *And ask those who are gathered together,*
> *Here in this cosmic temple of the Light,*
> *To assist me in Opening the Doors of the Palace of Light:*

> *I ask the Rules over the Inner Planes*
> *For the Matrix of the Winged Human Being.*
> *Let us connect ourselves with our highest spiritual quest*
> *And call up those forces that are our birth right.*
> *We ask the Gate of Eternity to open!*

Then the doors swing open and a spicy wind enters into the temple room. The entire space is filled with the wonderful smell of roses. From behind the doors a white appearance steps forward, carrying a bright flame in her hands. The entity stretches out her arms. The flame she brings floats towards the altar and remains hovering above it.

"Behold, I bring the essence of every spiritual human being, the Seed of Light. It connects each person with their highest goal in life through a Tear of the Sun. In every human being burns a Solar Teardrop, because in every person the highest light burns bright deep inside."

The white appearance makes a gesture above the clay baby and the Solar Teardrop changes into a sparkling star that remains hovering above its head.

Then the Lady of the Planetary Deva steps forward and speaks into the direction of the East:

We, who are the forerunners of humanity on their spiritual quest,
We have come together in this Temple of Light,
To connect ourselves with the Winged Human Being.
We offer our hearts to this holy altar.
While we walk the Path of Love,
We open the Spiritual Gateway to the Earth!

Also here the doors open and a second shining appearance floats forward and upholds a pyramid shaped rock crystal. The light penetrates it and causes rainbows to move through the entire temple space. The white entity speaks;

"Behold, I bring a looking glass. When a spiritual human being looks through this prism, searching the core of his life's questions, his mind will be filled will the colors of love and compassion. This glass contains the rainbow, the bridge between humanity and the Gods."

Now the Warrior-Monk rises. He opens his arms and addresses the South. His deep voice resonates and fills the entire space. He carries within himself the full meaning of the words he speaks, so that everyone inside feels the impact:

> *The Doors of Eternity open,*
> *Feel how a strong spiritual power flows into us.*
> *It helps us with the realization of our virtues,*
> *And the development of every talent that we own.*
> *Feel how this power becomes active at the highest spiritual level.*
> *We open the Gate of Fire!*

A third entity steps forward and upholds a wand. He steps towards the altar, and the staff disappears into the spine of the clay baby on the altar.
"Behold, I bring you the Axis Mundi, the staff that connects heaven and earth. This wand is a gift of the Gods and enables the Winged Human Being to link his earthly experiences for ever with the Wisdom of the Stars."
The Walker-Between-the-Worlds now rises and turns around self-assured to the Western Gate. He closes his eyes and with the utmost concentration he also speaks his invocation:

We work towards this goal, to realize it during our lives.
In this Temple of the Light we offer ourselves
To the Masters of the Inner Planes.
We open the Portals of Wisdom and welcome our teachers!

Now the double doors also open in the West. A fourth lightning entity appears, steps forward and speaks.

"Behold, I bring a mirror. When a spiritual person looks into this mirror, on his quest for his life's mission, he will fill himself with inspiration and wisdom. This mirror is the Window to Divinity. I bring you the face of your highest aspect, that part of yourself as you are seen by the Gods."

Then we all concentrate on the ceiling of the temple. A magical light shines through the stained glass picture of the mystical rose. The colors of the different glass segments slowly change into indigo blue and on the place where the Hebrew letters were engraved, now the nightly constellations of the zodiac appear. The planets move through space. I look upwards and my breath stocks, my eyes widen and I feel deep awe for the Greatness I perceive. Although I have been able to access this level earlier, I am deeply touched by the realization how small I am amidst of this vast beauty. My heart jumps at witnessing these mighty phenomena. Then I speak:

"Let us connect ourselves consciously with the Winged Human Being within us, the highest light of our soul." I stretch out my right hand above the altar and a ray of starlight falls into the stone of my ring. Six rays shoot forth form the star sapphire and they connect themselves with the six planets above my head. I contact the star of the ring with my heart, so that the starlight now also shoots forth from me. In my Sphere of Sensation the Interior Stars light up. "I wear this magical ring as a token of my covenant with the Highest Light, like the Sages of the Ages did throughout the times. I am the servant of that Light, of the Winged Human Being that lives in the depths of our souls." Then I chant the incantation:

> *Being that knows the essence of things,*
> *Of the past and of the future.*
> *Being that resonates in harmony with the Highest Light.*
> *Being that mirrors itself to the Highest Will.*
> *Being that knows the past and the future,*
> *That has access to what happened and has been forgotten;*
> *That knows what the future will bring.*
> *Being that knows how to read the Signs in Nature,*
> *Who knows the difference between false and true friends,*
> *I kneel and follow You as my guide.*

The Lady of the Planetary Deva follows my example. The stone at her hand flashes while she speaks the words. I listen, enjoy them and open my heart for the beauty she brings to the ritual on the sounds of her words:

> *I activate this Ring of Power to serve the Light*
> *And empower the Winged Human Being,*

That lives in the depths of the soul of humanity.
Thou who aren't enlightened in al manners and degrees;
Whether they speak as wind or weather,
As rivers or as oceans, as mammals or as humans.
Thou who advises me from your all-knowing wisdom,
I kneel and follow You as my guide.

The Warrior-Monk adds his words to ours and now three stars shine bright above the clay baby. I get goose skin when I feel the powers rushing through me and enjoy the words that he speaks:

Also I give my energy to the Star of Power;
To serve the Light and to empower the Winged Human Being,
Who lives in the depths of our species.
Who has access to sacred caves
And the treasures that are hidden within us.
Help us with the Alchemical work at hand;
Holy Angel, help us to melt the Metals,
Ora et Labora, I pray and work.
I kneel and follow You as my guide.

The Walker-Between-the-Worlds completes the ritual gesture above the altar. The four Magi make a cross of light by means of a ritual grip under the light of the rose. The words of the Walker-Between-the-Worlds make the magical work complete:

In me the Solar Teardrop awakens and I offer my services
To empower the Winged Human Being,
That lives in the depths of the soul of our species.
Who knows the true nature of all our visions,
Whether they appear in glass or crystal,
In caves or in sacred lakes,
In the air, in rings and circles, in wax and in fire,
In Sun and Moon and in the lines of our hands.
I listen to Your voice and follow Your instructions,
I will act according to the wisdom that You teach me,
I kneel and follow you as my guide.

The light in the room changes, the baby of clay changes color, its internal energies start to move and come to life. Apart from the heartbeat now, the breathing starts and suddenly the child opens its eyes. I look into its eyes and see that the right eye is golden yellow, and the left eye pearly grey.

"He has the eyes of the Sun and the Moon," the Warrior-Monk remarks.

"Beautiful," sighs the Lady of the Planetary Deva.

"The work for this evening has been done," the Walker-Between-the-Worlds remarks.

"Indeed I answer. "I am very curious how this will work out. Thank you, all of you, for giving your time.

"You are welcome High Priestess", they answer.

Then it is time to leave the astral space. After we have said our goodbyes, we withdraw from the Inner Worlds.

I take the usual route to return to my temple and reconnect with my body. I feel the stiffness because of the long and intensive session. But it was beautiful! My heart still glows from the beauty and the refined feelings. I walk to my office and change my ritual cloths for my evening gown. I make notes in my Grimoire, my magical book wherein I note down all the practical work; and collect pictures and diagrams. My hands gently flip through the leafs; I think back to all the work, the experiences that are written down here. It is a costly work that I will leave to my successors, the ones who will follow my path; they will be able to use it as their book of recipes.

*****

A few days later Jason is back in the Netherlands, his head is filled with images of the beautiful art and architecture he has seen in Florence. His diary is filled with new names, notes and email addresses for his coming projects in the medical scene. He is on his way to his appointment with Melusine, to talk about his experiences. He has reservations about this meeting. Will it be useful? Looking back he thinks it was rather paranoid of him to connect the funny dream with the ring. But Melusine reacted very open and asked him to describe his experiences in an email. She assured him that for her this was known territory and that she wanted to meet him to talk things through.

His GPS obviously lost its road; he notices that he is driving in circles. It reminds him of finding a way through a labyrinth. He does not find the right address and parks the car to ask for directions to a by passer. The man sends him through some of the very small streets right into the mediaeval part of the town. There Jason finds the building, next to a small canal. He knocks at the door. It is an old-fashioned door knocker, an iron ring shaped in the form of a mermaid.

*****

I hear the sound of the knocker and open the door. It is Jason and I ask him whether it was easy to find his way. He starts telling me about his adventures and losing all directions in my neighborhood. I answer him smiling I have heard more often that I obviously have a labyrinth in front of my house. We walk through the corridor with the black-and-white tiles. I take his coat and we go inside. The coffee is ready and stands at a side table. When Jason has looked around and taken a seat, I open the conversation about his adventures.

"I recognize your experiences, Jason, they make perfect sense to me", I say. "You are waking up."
"What do you mean by waking up?" Jason answers.
"You are waking up to the Inner Worlds", I answer. I see Jason's face change into one big question mark.
"Most people are asleep for their Inner Life. They live their lives, do their jobs and are completely satisfied when their days follow a

normal pattern. They are extremely happy when they are not hit by big disasters. A nice house, a family, a dog, a beautiful car and a career. But some people get in touch with a deeper layer of reality. These people go through a crisis in the middle of their lives. It starts with the confrontation with consequences of the choices they have made up to that point in their lives. Superficially, this expansion of consciousness resembles a midlife crises. But it is not the same, because it does not necessarily come at that age. This crisis goes deeper, because it is an expansion of consciousness. Jung called it the Metanoia, a mental transformation that marks the second half of life in a limited group of people. They start to experience a strange and special type of energy rushing through their bodies. Nowadays this is sometimes called 'Kundalini-energy'. It enables you to make essential choices. It offers you the possibility to not only lead an intellectually and materially fulfilled life, but to become spiritually enlightened. It is a fundamental choice; do you take the quest for wisdom, or do you remain satisfied in foolishness? Do you wake up for the Inner Planes, or do you remain sleeping?

Meta-noia, the word comes from Greek and means 'under-spirit'. It is an old word that means sub-consciousness. You have all the signs of the awakening and expansion of consciousness. What do you want Jason? Are you willing to go through this inner process? Or do you turn down your chance to get access to the spiritual reality? At the beginning this can be frightening, because your entire worldview is turned upside down. But I know excellent methods to help people like you, to guide them through this process. When you use ancient and tested methods as guidelines, you arrive in a world of richness. A world that is known to just a few people. Most people remain sleepers.

In the old days everyone at least knew about the existence of this alternate reality and thus this Inner Richness was easy accessible for everyone. But during the Age of Enlightment the world of logic became dominant and the wealth of the inner worlds became ridiculed, on behalf material wealth and intellect.

"Nowadays only a small percentage of humanity makes the choice to access this spiritual reality. Most seekers have almost no support around them. They are scared, feel isolated from the normal world, and turn their back to the Inner Worlds. Society has declared this world 'taboo' and calls her a 'waste of time, an 'illusion that doesn't make the chimney smoke.' They think it is a floaty dream world, but this is caused because most of the seekers can no longer find the proper entrance into this world of richness. They lose their way on the Inner Planes and search without direction through the shadow worlds. They get lost; meanwhile they become alienated from the daily world, and run around in circles like in a mirror labyrinth.

"The experiences that you have, Jason, the physical reactions, the feeling of growing larger than your body, the strange dreams, the energy zigzagging through your body, the bright colors and the golden light—all of these are wake-up signs. You are one of the few people who are allowed to develop your inner worlds if you want."

"After what you told me just now, this appears to be a great risk," Jason answers.

"The risk is that you will never experience your life the same," I tell him. "You might find it strange or scary in the beginning.

Inevitably there will be some friends and acquaintances that will have trouble with your choice. That can become painful. The profit is that you will develop a rich and adventurous inner life. To develop real self-confidence and become firmly rooted into the core of your being. You open up to a world where real miracles happen, where you are being led by mysterious coincidences. It is a life of astonishing quests, full of goose skin realizations about the nature of life and the meaning of your existence. A world of richness, unlimited possibilities, of refined feelings and unworldly beauty."

Jason is quiet. He listens and I can see at his face that he goes through all kinds of conflicting emotions. "I find it very interesting, but I have no overview," he answers. "I know that weird things are going on in my body. I know that my dreams are very different from the dreams I used to have. But to turn my world upside down because of these experiences... What will happen when I do nothing?"

I smile at him. "That is difficult to say, but one thing I know for sure and that is that this process will continue for a while. You can of course choose to go through it on your own and run the risk of getting lost in the maze, taking the risk getting trapped in the illusions. You can also choose – at least temporary – to connect with people who know this process and work with it. Then you are no longer alone and you can observe how they handle the process. When you don't like it, you leave and find your own way."

"How do I find out where they meet?" Jason asks.

"Oh that is very simple," Melusine answers, "tonight one of my groups meet. This group is researching and they are full of questions. When you feel like it, you can join us for this meeting."

"Do you head these types of groups? What kind of person are you, Melusine?" Jason asks.

"I have made it to my mission to guide people who research the Inner Worlds. Call me a tour guide," I answer him smiling.

Jason and I walk to the meeting room. In about half an hour the visitors will arrive. My right-hand, Wolf, enters. We need some time to prepare the room for the lecture. First of all I cleanse the room energetically. Wolf prepares the flip over and gathers felt-tip pens. For me no power point presentations. I teach after another manner. While I talk I project images into the surrounding space that are picked up subconsciously by the visitors.

Wolf starts to fill the room with a subtle scent. I ignite a few beautiful candles and put some flowers in a vase. Jason watches while I am busy with the preparations and asks me whether he can help. "It would be fantastic when you could help preparing the coffee," I smile, thankful. That is always a good sign, when the people realize that they can contribute to the whole. That means that they are able to rise above their individual level and that is always a sign of a healthy inner potential.

The doorbell rings, and one by one old and new faces enter the venue. I greet all those nice people. "How is your son doing, did he put up with the flue? Did you pass your exam?" It is always a nice and cozy welcoming ceremony with warm embraces. I feel how my heart opens, while I tune into all these different persons. People who, from their busy lives, sacrifice some hours of their personal time to visit these evenings. Some of them live nearby and hardly need to travel. Others literally journey for hours to attend these meetings. All sacrifice some of their costly time to work at their spiritual lives. I look around and observe the group that enters and I think, "These people are really investing in themselves."

The barstools slowly fill up and at one of the tables an interesting discussion arises. Jason listens while the present persons exchange their opinions.

Luke starts the conversation. "Many people who are developing themselves spiritually find it difficult to explain to their environment what they are doing. Their peers consider this to be a strange hobby. Do you recognize that?"

Janine answers, "I know that they consider this to be strange, but I can explain it. Often it turns out that they have had spiritual experiences themselves. On top of that … this is who I am and it makes me happy, they need to take me for what I am, and when they have questions I will answer them!"

Richard continues, "It can be explained up to a certain point, but there comes a moment that others who are not on the same path can no longer follow you. From that point on I stopped explaining, because it is useless."

Gea nods her head, and Janine continues. "Indeed there is a point where it is no longer possible to explain. When you start the training in the Mystery schools you don't learn common knowledge. People really need to dig into that stuff and say yes to their experiences."

Jason thinks, he has never heard of Mystery schools before. Nice fairy tale!

Hilde ponders, and then she remarks, "It gets difficult because people consider it to be a threat … everything is fine, as long as they don't need to change ... In my environment people prefer to be brooders instead of allowing the thought that things could get better and they could be doing better. I understand them, because when you start following this path, there is no way back," she answers smiling.

Luke continues, "You have all chosen to follow this path. Others remain standing in the entrance. The fear being casted off, or no longer being taken seriously. How did you get through?"

Hilde calls out enthusiastically, "I have always been connected, I always knew it somewhere ... I have waited until the times became better, until I could handle it and make it stronger and more stable."

Henry breathes deeply and frowns his eyebrows. He rubs his forehead. "I never had this fear. That is because I always was 'different' because of my hypersensitivity. By all this I have learned to go for it, no matter what 'they' think about it. But I can imagine that this feels differently for everyone."

Jason listens carefully. This is a complete new world for him. He remembers from his childhood to be an outsider as well. But he has closed that part of himself.

Ramon now continues, "I just went down this road, because it felt right. Finally I have learned to be quieter about it. Sometimes this is hard, because there is always the person that tries to get you, but I consider that to be a lesson of the universe," he says joking. "The more I felt at home with myself, the quieter I become in my head and in my body; I feel like coming home."

Luke knots his head in thoughts, turns around to Henry and remarks, "There are a lot of spiritual people who feel 'differently.' Welcoming the tradition in your life feels like coming home, finally. In spite of that there are many that feel torn apart—torn between two worlds that are sometimes conflicting. Gradually you learn to remain to stay centered in my power, because your inner resources have become clearer."

Jason thinks that there is a complete market of magazines that deal with these topics. Maybe tonight will give him an idea for an article that he can sell.

"I recognize this," says David while he leans forward over the bar, making himself visible to the others. "I used to suffer from it as well. But recently society developed more tolerance and I experience more recognition and reassurance, instead of the pointing of fingers to the forehead."

Mary quietly remarks, "Most of the time I don't speak about it."

Luke grins. "I have jokingly said that many of us have ended up 'into the closet.'"

Mary agrees. "I am in that closet. Sometimes I come out for a quick moment, mumble something; my environment disagrees or doubts it. Sooner or later it turns out to be accurate. Seers, feelers and creators are deadly scared for all those who have closed themselves off."

"Hmmm," Jason thinks, "that is an interesting quote."

Henry now gets emotional. "There are certain television shows that are not helpful, because they only confirm preconceived opinions!" he sounds angry.

Mary raises her hands in despair. "I have seen parts of a paranormal show on television. It could be considered humor, if it was not so sad."

Ramon agrees that this type of programs is a waste of time. "They are based on the presumptions of the masses about us. They don't have any relation to what we are and what we do, or what we can accomplish when we train or abilities," he says while lowering his shoulders.

Luke says, "You do not need to evangelize. It should be normal to be respected because of who you are and what you are about!"

Slowly the hall fills up with people, and I withdraw to prepare my lecture and the exercise of this evening. A last view in the mirror, I look at my speech and hear how Luke announces me. I enter into the hall. I take a deep breath and step on the stage. I see Jason sitting at the first row, and swiftly greet him.

"Good evening everyone, how nice that you have come with so many this evening. Tonight I have a special topic on my program, on request of some of you. But I know for a fact that this is a topic that people want to hear more about. The theme of this evening is: How to develop yourself in a solid way as a spiritual being?

"Of course it is fantastic that nowadays you are free to choose your spiritual path. The mystics of former ages looked forward to the coming of the New Age. Nowadays you do not need to follow any religion; you can believe what you want. With the invention of the Internet, a constant current of information about every thinkable spiritual topic has become accessible. All spiritual knowledge is public and available. You do not need to acknowledge the authority of any teacher. The gurus are gone!" Everyone starts to laugh, but it gets quiet very quickly. "The universe belongs to everyone and thus the universal knowledge as well. With a little bit of luck you remember a former incarnation as a high priest. You only need to plug in your spiritual antennae in the socket of the cosmos, and you can download all the Knowledge of the All."

"So, away with the courses where you are being brainwashed, gone with the sects and the dogmatic religions. In this time and age we no longer need an intermediary between ourselves and the Divine..."

The people laugh and nod. "Yes, exactly!"

"You can observe it everywhere around you, in the spiritual subculture everyone has become the guru of their private universe. People channel books, with the lessons of the Gods inside. But where does it lead you? What is the profit when you turn your subconscious mind upside down and market the content? What is the goal of spiritual development? Do you notice that around you? That people lose solid ground under their feet? In society they do their jobs, and in their spare time they lead a completely schizophrenic other life. As an undercover mystic they search for friends on the Internet. And there is an overload of information about 'spiritual development'. Ripe and green dump their knowledge on the web. How to divide the wheat from the chaff when you are a beginner? People get uprooted because they have no idea how to attach their inner experiences to their daily lives. The different worlds remain separated: the outer world and their mystical experiences. What makes it even more complex is the lame are helping the blind. Everyone holds their personal opinion for The Truth and they start a guru-war. Where do you find the spiritual training that was accessible for true seekers in this day and age, the knowledge that was available throughout the ages?"

The people in the hall move restless. People quickly exchange thoughts and move on their chairs. Someone raises and asks, "Is that knowledge still available?"

Another person remarks that it is just a nice hobby to spend an evening with friends.

I look around and search for eye contact with some of the attendees. I see raised eyebrows. People are making notes and some of them start a discussion with their neighbor. Jason also looks around, like he expects the answer to appear from somewhere. Then I continue my speech:

"Luckily this knowledge is still available. But it is extremely difficult to find, when you don't know what to look for. The training is still being offered, like in the old days, from mouth-to-ear, from teacher to student. That means that the people who have completely finished the training program, teach what they have learned to their carefully selected group of students. When they have passed on everything they know, also these students become masters in their turn, and educate the next generation of students. When this goes on from generation to generation, this is called a Lineage. In every generation there is a group of people who pass on the knowledge about spiritual development and translate it so that it can be understood through the times.

"The average seeker thinks that this knowledge is available through the Internet and in books. The marketing-guru's scream that initiations are for sale, or that you are already enlightened. The true teachers have a less popular message to tell. I want to introduce you to the words of an initiate from the 15th century. His name is Giovanni Pico della Mirandola. His words are still important:

> *The Creator said: "People, I have placed you into the center of the world: nether in Heaven, nor on Earth. We have not made you mortal or immortal. You are responsible for your choices yourselves, because you are the sculpture of your life. You can mold yourself in any form you wish. You can choose to grow your lower nature and become a brute. You can also lead your soul upward; let it grow to the higher spheres of existence that are divine. It is your decision what you want to become.*[v]

I look around the hall and gauge the atmosphere. "You can hear that this old master emphasizes the free will of humanity. Then he explains the difference between people who call up chaotic spiritual forces and people who contact the higher forces of goodness deliberately and consciously and in this way serve nature; people who see their live as an art or a science. These people are looking for the deepest secret of nature. They bring light to mysterious places, they make the miracles visible that are lying dormant, ready to sprout in the womb of nature and in the secret Treasure Houses of the Divine. Then he continues:

> *"Like a farmer he connects the grape tendrils with the grapevine and in a similar way the Magus connects the Heaven with the*

> *Earth; he connects the lower regions of talents with the higher regions.*[vi]

This type of development aims to cause experiences with the transcendental world yourself. In this way you gain experience, knowledge that ripens into an adult relationship with the Inner Worlds. The choice is yours: what road do you prefer?"

And with this question I leave my public. Dindrane comes walking towards me and I ask her to prepare the room for meditation. I walk to Jason to see how he is doing. He is torn apart. I read his thoughts. One half of him regards this topic a puppet theatre. *How can I explain to my friends what I have been doing this evening, and what it brought to me?'* Then he straightens his back. *'These are a bunch of weirdo's who throw an alternative party; I have visited more strange places in my life.* Then he feels the undeniable longing to explore that long forgotten side of him. *What do these people share? There is something mutual that they share, something that resembles an answer that I am searching, but I have no clue what it is, and where it will bring me.* So he straightens his shoulders and says that he is doing fine, and that he holds the meeting for interesting.

I pet him encouragingly on the shoulder. "After the break we will do a meditation together that will help you further." I sign Dindrane and ask her to guide Jason during the break. Then I withdraw to contact the Inner Planes. I ask the Eternal Wisdom to guide me in what needs to be said right now.

The Primordial Hill - meditation

Then I return to the hall. Dindrane meanwhile has taken care of the rearrangement of the chairs. We now sit in a circle. I take my place and ask everyone to sit upright and close the eyes.

"Breathe deeply a few times, relax and let go. Leave all your worries behind in your daily life and turn your views inwards, go to that inner space where everything is good and beautiful, exactly as it should be. Contact the Cosmos above you and admire the beauty of a velvet black starry night. Look how the Eternal Lights sparkle like diamonds on an evening gown; it is the robe of the Goddess of the Night.

"Experience how from the Endless Emptiness a hand stretches out to you. In the palm you see a shining star. The Goddess of the Night carefully brings a star down; it hovers above your head. You hear the soft whispering of her voice while she speaks to you. 'This is your star, beloved child. It helps you to connect with the highest aspects of your being, the part of you that knows why you are here. She is a light that guides you and when you pay close attention, you can hear her deep inside when she speaks to you.'

"Feel how from this star a lightning flash rushes through you. The ray enters through the top of your head. Feel it scintillating. She radiates so brightly that a light awakens in your heart. At first it is a subtle flame, but slowly it increases in intensity, so that also there a bright star starts to shine. The star above your head twinkles, and suddenly a second lightning flash comes down. This time it penetrates your spine and strikes the earth beneath your feet. Now you are completely surrounded with light. Through your feet you feel how the lightning flash zigzags downwards, penetrating the Inner Earth. It is like you grow roots. Then the Earth responds and a wave of Earth Fire now ascends through your spine. It rises to your heart level. In your thoughts you stretch out your hands over the horizon and feel how the light flashes around you. You appear to get wings. Then you see it, right opposite of you: a big eye in a triangle. It stares at you and from the eye six rays of light shoot in all directions. Each ray has its own color. Four Hebrew letters dance around the Eye. You get bigger, while the roots under your feet start to grow and deeply penetrate into the Inner Earth. The Eye comes towards you. You feel the pressure on your third eye increasing. It starts to beat and to pull. There appears to be a heat coming from the Eye. Then suddenly it is as if you are captured in a whirlwind and the Eye is sucked by the forces coming from your forehead. It nestles itself in your brain, in between your two eyes. You notice that the intensity by which you can see on the Inner Planes now increases gigantically. All your senses are involved, your hearing, your touch, your inner knowing, everything is intensified.

It is as if you have arrived in a three-dimensional movie, in which you are the center. You clearly hear a bellowing inner voice: 'For Your Eye Only.'

"Then it starts to rain. It pours down in huge quantities. Everything around you gets flooded. Big foam heads form on the tops of waves and you can clearly see the appearances of animals. Serpents, dragons, running dogs and scorpion-people. Amidst of raging storms, fiery rams and fish-people appear before your inner eye. Large dangerous animals. Meanwhile the entire land is under water. You stand amidst of a whirling mass of water. The four Hebrew letters dance around the Eye. Each of the four letters changes into a being of fire. The fire beings turn around and form a vertical chain from Heaven to Earth, and together they create a huge pillar. The pillar comes towards you and you become one with the pillar: a voice echoes through space. *Do you know that Divine Consciousness takes on form; that it nestles itself in matter? You, yes, you! You are a God in a human body. Go and create, create your own reality!*

"Witness how from the Eye seven rays illuminate the landscape. The rays create a prism and in this rainbow of color a pyramid of light forms itself. Clearly you see that it is three-dimensional. Climb the pyramid, until you reach the top. See how the lightning strikes again, witness two large wings of light stretching out and covering the entire horizon. Then the Four Hebrew Letters separate from you. They are fire beings, angels; they cleave through space and reach the ends of the horizon. The Yod in front of you, the Vav behind you. The two Heh's at your left and right side. The fire beings ignite the lights of four Watchtowers; they give directions and drive off the darkness. See how the waters separate; the salt water sinks down to the bottom of the pyramid. The sweet waters withdraw to the heavens. And you are standing amidst of a hill of light. A bird comes flying towards you. A golden falcon lands on your shoulder. The water now calms and streams into four riverbeds, calmly flowing, creating a natural protection around your interior landscape.

"Slowly the water sinks and is canalized by the riverbeds. Now that the water is calmer, you see that the animals get friendlier and form a big circle around you. A ram, a bull, twins, a crab, a lion, a virgin ... Libra, Scorpion, Sagittarius, Capricorn, Aquarius and Pisces. The animals of the zodiac will lead you and help you to gain mastership over your life.

"Hear the sound that now echoes over the landscape. *You have arrived at the center of your world, as a mediator in between the forces of heaven and earth. You now almost hold the tools in your hands to create your own world. You need one more thing to do, and that is this:*

"From the eye rolls a ball of light and you pick it up with both hands. At the moment you hold it, it shrinks together and takes on the shape of a seed. *Plant this stone as a seed on your land, and you will be surprised,* says the voice.

"You follow the directions and plant the seed on the top of the hill. When you have done that, you give it a sip of water: water of the tears that you shed in sorrow, water of the tears that you cry of joy.

"Now it is time to leave the inner landscape. Let the images slowly blur. Collect them into a big cloud of inspiration and draw it together in your heart. Breathe a few times, stretch your muscles and slowly open your eyes. You are back in the now and you feel fabulous. Reconnect yourself with your body and open your eyes, fully awake and alert."

I look around and see how everyone slowly starts to awaken from the meditation. People start to move and stretch. They rise and walk in the direction of the coffee and tea. I also stand and follow them. I chat with people I pass and see how Jason and Dindrane are talking animated.

"I expect the process to continue more harmoniously now," I say to Jason. "I would appreciate it being informed how you are doing. Of course, you can always email me or give a call in case of an emergency.

Jason looks at Melusine. He gets caught in her intense glance and cuts himself loose from it. He thanks her and assures that he will most certainly contact her, at latest in fourteen days.

He observes Melusine's movements when she hugs her students and says goodbye. Then she leaves the space and disappears.

Jason says goodbye to Dindrane and thanks her for her explanations that she has given him throughout the evening. He puts on his coat and thinks about what has been said and about the riddle that keeps him busy: *Who is Melusine*? But is that the right question? At moments she almost is unearthly...'

*****

THE WATER SPELLS

4

THE WATER SPELLS

EBB

Direciton is relative,
Withdrawal brings progress
By reversing the goal.

"Jason, we are done," is the completely unexpected message at the telephone. Jason starts sweating. As his heart beats quickly, an intense pain flows through his entire body, and his heart bleeds because of the unexpected message. Joan tells him that she does not want to continue their relationship. It is as if he is hit by a tank. . Jason has difficulties accepting the message Joan tells him: "I have met someone else and fell in love. I want to move on with this guy, Jason. I want to have children, and my time is limited to develop a relation with someone who wants them too. I don't want to wait any longer until you might be ready for them. I is useless to try to solve this. Our lives are moving in different directions!"

She tells him that she will contact him later to share her thoughts about their house and the division of the furniture. The message hits him in the stomach. Somehow Jason still hoped that a short break would rekindle the fire of the importance of their relationship. That the warm mutual feelings would win over her wish for children; that they could find another basis to continue. This hope has now disappeared. What next? He ambles aimlessly through the streets. Walking, walking, just to be among people, search for a distraction. But the world of today looks grey and the world of the average person appears to be boring and superficial. People are busy in an artificial world, wherein luck is defined as having the newest mobile phone and the amount of followers on Facebook. Jason feels like a lonely island in a moving mass of people. A mass that only cares about their own small world. There is no distraction and he feels his jaws pressing together and his hands become fists in his back pockets.

Move on, move on ... He takes the car and drives to the coast. He wants to feel the endless horizon. He drives full throttle and in no time arrives at the small town near the sea. When he has parked the car, he walks along the fishing-house. His footsteps sound hollow on the cobbles. As he looks out over the water it starts to rain and he cannot get rid of his energy. He walks up to one of the round bridges and looks out over the water. He feels the urge to challenge the elements. The wind sweeps over the water and the rain comes down in torrents from the sky.

But it doesn't really move him. He looks over the ferocious sea and holds the railing of the bridge.

Foundation? That does not exist. Why do people want to hold together? Does one choose for a child, or is a child the glue to keep the pair together? Having children or not, it really is a fundamental choice. Will my friends understand that I do not want them? People around me say that having children within an established relationship is a natural outcome of that relation. They consider that to be an unwritten right. When the relation with Joan ends because of my refusal, will they think that there is something wrong with me? Is there something wrong? Do I have a bonding problem? Is the luxury that we have nowadays, to have sex without children, compatible with our essential nature? The choice between fertility and sterility is essential and irreversible: do these laws only apply to physical children, or also to the fruits of my work? All these thoughts shoot through Jason's head.

Then, as a sledgehammer blow, the next problem hits him. *The house!* Bought in a too expensive time, a time when everyone thought that trees grow into the heavens. The depth of the mortgage is no longer equal to its value, due to the plotting of the financial industry, 'creating' money out of nothing.

He has promised his future salary for the coming twenty-five years to the people of the bank. But this money, earned by honest hard working is no longer covered! It has changed into figures in a computer, and those figures are being manipulated. But he needs to work real blood, sweat, and tears to resolve this virtual depth.

What is the real value of money? Money used to be a resource to exchange valuable things.

What is my value? Am I a money-making machine for a billionaire? How do I retrieve my power? How would it be to sail in these weather circumstances, to measure my strength with nature? All these thoughts rush through his head.

He walks to the rental business of the sailing vessels and asks whether it is possible to rent a boat. The boatman assures him that the weather is too bad to sail, and that it is irresponsible to leave the shore. Jason walks further and leaves the town. He walks to a place where he has a full sight on the water. He sees the bending reed in the rushing wind, hears the waves splashing against the shores, and feels the greatness of the landscape. He looks into the endless distances of whirling foaming waves as the raging wind pulls at his cloths and freezes his fingers. He feels the power of the wind; *how powerful is that wind, how mighty are those waters.* He soaks in all the physical sensations. A lightning flash cuts through his spine and a heat zigzags through his body.

Through the massive grey clouds a ray of sunlight hits the water. It reflects and forms a path of light over the whirling waves. The clouds drift along on the chasing wind. They resemble faces. The clouds become more compact and form nebulas. The sunlight shines through and the clouds illuminate from within. On the pathway of sunlight a radiating figure appears, dressed in a robe of sea green and blue. It resembles a ghostly appearance. Jason shakes his head and rubs his eyes. *What is this?* Filled with disbelief he watches the phenomena that take place before his very eyes. The wind rushes around him and suddenly Jason hears a voice talking to him:

"Jason, it is time you learn to sail the Cosmic Ocean. Learn to achieve Mastership over the Element of Water. Water is the element that you need to control, in order to achieve entrance to the Otherworld. Water carries you into the world of the Unseen, the world of feeling, of inner knowing, of intuition. Water is the realm of the spirit, the place to contact your resources, where you can meet your ancestors. It is the dwelling place of Gods and Angels. There you will retrieve the power of your soul, Jason, learn to Walk on Water!"

The figure comes walking towards him over the Path of Light. Clearly Jason sees the bare feet in the sandals. The appearance stretches out his hands to Jason in a welcoming gesture.

Jason exclaims aloud: "What is happening to me?"

The appearance speaks reassuringly, "Be brave, do not be scared." And again it holds out his hand. Like in a dream, Jason looks at the face and melts away in the love that radiates from the figure. An intense longing to come home, to feel safe whirls up inside of him and he grasps the outstretched hand and steps on the water. Then he fully realizes what he is doing and feels his shoes sinking in the mud. The shock awakens him from his trance and his heart misses one beat.

"Have trust," the appearance says, "there is no need for doubt, and you will learn to navigate the Seas of the Otherworld. It is an art that can be learned without danger. Contact your physical teacher, because there is a work of greatness waiting for you to be accomplished." Then the clouds draw together again and Jason realizes that he is standing with his feet in the water. The sea slowly withdraws, it is ebb …

Shocked, Jason walks back to the occupied world. What is the nature of his experience? He trudges through the loose sand until he reaches a tavern. Deeply involved in his own thoughts he walks in. *What is wrong with me? Did the shock of Joan's message upset me so much that I am getting hallucinations? Did the wiring in my head get crossed? What was this insane experience about? Creepy, very creepy…! But was it really that scary? There was so much love coming from that appearance.*
In his thoughts Jason repeats the memory like a video camera playing the scene again. He hears the words echo through his mind. Jason searches for a place where he can recover from his experiences. The beach café has a conservatory. Through the glass windows is a great view on the sea while providing shelter. There he sits down, takes out his mobile and calls Melusine.

*****

It is halfway in the afternoon when my phone rings unexpectedly. I see that it is Jason. I am amidst of a consultation with Eagle about the developments within the group. We evaluate the situation and discuss what every one of the participants needs for their development in the near future. "I am curious about what he has to say," I say to Eagle. "It is an unusual time for a telephone call."
"That is the bloke that found your ring, isn't it?" Eagle asks.

I shake my head: "He is of the greatest importance for the Great Work that we started, Eagle! He needs to sail through that difficult phase at the start of his development."

Then I pick up the phone. "Melusine..." I get a garbled story, I squeeze my eyes, put my teeth together, and uncover them in a grimace. I shake my head 'no' to Eagle and bring my hand to my mouth. I listen carefully and frown while I listen. I hear the underlying disbelief and confusion.

"Where are you now? Let me have a quick consult," I put my hand on the telephone. "He has had a breakthrough and arrived at a restaurant on the beach."

"Do you need to go there?" Eagle asks.

"I think I would rather go there than ask him to drive to me," I answer.

"Shall I drive you there?" Eagle asks.

"That would be fantastic, Eagle, but I need to speak to him alone."

"No problem, Melusine. We can finish our conversation in the car. And when I have dropped you off, I'll drive to Gabriella, and inform her about the program coming Sunday on behalf of the Western Quarter. When you are finished you give me a ring and I will collect you."

"You are a darling," I say to Eagle. I put the telephone to my ear again and say to Jason: "Give me the address of the venue, and I'll come to you. I will be there within half an hour."

*****

We park the car. Eagle accompanies me as we walk to the sea. We plod though the loose sand, and then we walk the wooden foot board towards the beach tent. We enter and look around. There I see Jason, sitting in front of the window, with a view on the sea. I walk towards him and embrace him wholeheartedly. I introduce him to Eagle:

"Jason, this is Eagle. He is a member of the team of people that collaborate with me. He was with me when you called and was nice enough to drive me here."

Jason looks at Eagle, an elderly man in his sixties. He is long and slender and wears glasses. His hair is light brown and he has a quiet smile. "Hey, Jason, chap, good to meet you," he speaks with an authentic Amsterdam dialect. "Did I meet you at the meditation evening a while ago? I saw you talking to Dindrane, if I am not mistaken."

"Yes, indeed. That was an interesting evening. Do you organize these evenings often?" Jason asks.

"Yes, every week, and each time a part of the regular team is present," Eagle answers. "But I will leave you in the competent hands of Melusine, because I have understood that you have a lot to exchange."

"Send my greetings to Gabriella," I say to Eagle. He raises his hand for an answer, turns around, and leaves the beach tent.

The Winding Waterway

The road of the intuition

I order a cup of coffee and look over the beach to the sea. The sun now shines gently over the water as far as I can see. I take in the landscape. In my mind I let myself drift on the clouds and observe their shapes. For a moment I become one with the endless space in front of me, I hear the sounds of seagulls, and taste the salty taste of heavy sea air.

"That was an extraordinary experience you had. Do you have an explanation for what you witnessed?" I ask.

"I was completely disorientated," Jason answers. "I hold it for dangerous that I react so intensely on the bad news that I was already expecting. I feel like walking on quicksand, and that my life will fall apart, and me with it."

"I understand that you got extremely scared, but I have the feeling that something else is going on as well, something related to the awakening process that you are in. Can you tell me as detailed as possible what happened?" I ask.

Jason starts to talk; how the clouds separated and the sun created a path of light. About the appearance that walked towards him and talked to him. On my request he repeats the words of the entity as precise as possible:

"Have trust, you will learn to navigate the Seas of the Otherworld. It is an art that can be learned without danger. Contact your physical teacher, because there is a work of greatness waiting for you to be accomplished."

"So that is what I did immediately. I walked to this place and called you right away."

I am happy with this sign of trust, and give him an encouraging pat on his hand. "I think you have had a vision, Jason. You met Titurel, the Fisherking. That is a spiritual guide." I look at the face opposite of me and see one big question mark.

"I will explain it to you," I say. "Did you ever hear of the sixth sense?" Jason raises his eyebrows because he does not believe in this stuff. He nods a little bit unsure.

"Well in fact, that is not one sense, but all your senses have a possibility to receive psychically. Within our tradition we call them the Inner Senses. What is called in popular language 'the sixth sense' can be trained, and this capacity is used to experience the Otherworld. What you went through this afternoon is that you have been granted a peep-through in the Otherworld. Because all your Inner Senses were involved, an experience like this becomes extremely realistic. That you have experienced this in your stage of the awakening process is extraordinary. Your personal crisis probably made you more vulnerable and that caused this experience to become so overpowering. Many people experience such phenomena, but in the first instance is mostly less intense as yours. When you start to train yourself, these kind of experiences will come less unexpectedly and you will develop methods in how to deal with them, how to give this special reality a place in your life. Finally, you will be able to make a conscious contact with this realm when you need information from that layer of reality. But first I will try to explain some things about this topic." I start my explanation while I constantly check whether Jason is able to process my information. I survey his reactions while I am speaking to him:

"You observe the world with your five senses; hearing, touching, smelling, tasting, and seeing. They are five different states of consciousness that help you register everything you experience in your life. Through your physical body you register temperature, hunger, danger, and so on. By means of your smell you receive – on top of the signals that inform you whether the air that you breathe is healthy – also sexual signals and more information. Your senses open not only the outer world, but also give access to an inner world of experiences. On top of that you also have the ability to reason. This is sometimes called the 'digital sense.'"

Jason nods, that does not sound unreasonable. I continue: "But we do not register everything with our senses. For example, there are sounds that we cannot hear, but dogs can. We cannot see infrared and ultraviolet blue, but we can measure them."

I bend forward to Jason. He listens intently. He looks at me. I can hear his thoughts; *She is a very special lady.* When he looks into my eyes he will sense my inner world of mysticism. I send him a wave of healing energy that will change his feelings. I see how it penetrates him, curing and caressing him. It is as if the sun starts to shine again from the inside out. I hear him thinking: *Who is she? There is something about her that is almost not of this world.*

I continue: "Most people trust their five senses completely. But in fact that is a limitation, because when you develop more sensitivity, you start to register impressions that are not limited to the five senses. You learn to use your senses, not only to receive impressions from the outer world, but also from the Inner Worlds. You learn to refine them, and use them as sensitive antennae for the Otherworld. That Otherworld is the world of the interconnected consciousness of the entire earth and her relation to the cosmos. She consists of psychic impressions and invisible connections, caused by empathic relations. She connects the past with the future. The Otherworld consists of psychic energy fields that draw together like clouds. It is like a downpour of contracting consciousness falling down over us as the Spirit of the Time, causing all actual events to happen. The Otherworld is a world of unlimited consciousness. When you become more sensitive, it opens slowly your ability to receive information from these psychic areas and your inner senses translate these impressions in language, images, and in physical feelings."

Jason's hair rises. A shiver goes down his spine like he instinctively recognizes the reality that is explained to him.

"The ability to perceive more than just the physical reality accelerates in times of crisis; it has always been an important survival skill for humanity. To make it even more clear: it is the inner radar that informs animals to flight in time, long before we are able to perceive a natural disaster. But that inner radar is also important under normal circumstances. Because our modern society emphasizes only the material reality, the antennae for the Otherworld has become covered under dust for most humans. Imagine the consequences of this fact: when we no longer access our inner radar, we become more and more alienated of our healthy feelings. When we do not have access to the transpersonal reality, we lose a part of our soul. We suffer because we are cut loose from our resources of inspiration, happiness, and health; we get separated from our divine spark. We lose the feeling to orientate ourselves to those inner coordinates that connect us with the Matrix of Harmony of the Universe. We lose our connection to the Axis Mundi; the world-axis, the center from which you can perceive what happens inside of you and outside. When you are no longer connected to the Axis Mundi, your relation between you and the Earth gets disturbed and comes between yourself and the transpersonal higher levels of consciousness. Your Inner Senses are the organs that connect you to the divine part of yourself, your soul. That higher part of yourself is connected to the All. It is the part of you that enables you to get experiences of true beauty. It is your antennae that enable you to perceive the beauty of the people around you and of nature. Spiritual awakening does exactly that: you become more sensitive and reconnect with beauty, with sustainable values, with human dignity. It always appears as a crisis and the awareness about the less comfortable sides of the process.

"You get into connection with Inner Knowing and with true compassion. Apparent contradictions are resolved and you enter into a state of flow: that is a creative outburst in which what you do is in complete harmony with who you are. In this way you can build a life for yourself that is in alignment with your true nature. Often the question about the meaning of life is depicted as a question of luxury. But I say that it comes forth from a longing to realize ourselves completely." I look at Jason. I see a longing expression on his face; he sits, leaning forward, and drinks in every word I speak.

"That is a way of looking and observing that is completely new for me," Jason says. "What are the consequences of us being cut loose from this information?"

"Our planet breathes this consciousness of unity, and for us humans it is extremely important to be in tune with this harmony. Most people are deaf for the higher reality of nature around us. This is one of the causes of environmental pollution, a disaster of an unpreceded volume! Cultural differences run the risk of escalating into conflicts. Also spiritual poverty and the extinction of animal species are related to this problem. Look around you, Jason, at what is being obscured behind the scenes, what is being shoved under the rug! World leaders are not chosen because of their ethical reliability, but based on the ability to mask the inhuman sides of their decisions. They are completely dissociated from their deeper nature. When we learn again to breathe in and out on the spiritual tides of our planet, the work that we will be doing will be in harmony with the Planetary Deva again."

Gradually the heavens changes color, the sun slowly sinks into the sea. The clouds turn red while their background changes into a deepening blue color. Everything is mirrored in the waters. When the blue changes into purples, the sea reflects these colors as well. The golden disk sinks slowly below the horizon and reflects its last rays on the ocean, and then it disappears.

"The blue hour has begun," I say. The first stars turn up. I point towards one of the clearest lights that now appear. "That is Venus, she follows the Sun." The light of the lighthouse is now turned on, a ray of clear light cleaves thought the evening blue.

"Come, let's walk along the beach," I say to Jason. We walk along the coastline over the wed sand. "Look at this splendid view. There is no visible border between the sea and the heaven. Look at the movements of the stars. Every star follows the path of the sun. They arise in the east and sink down in the west. Then they disappear under the horizon and follow the path of the Sun-at-Midnight. To the visible eye they make a gigantic spiral movement." I point towards the south. "Look, there you see the well-known constellations. It appears to be a meaningless series of sparkling lights, but the patterns were connected to mythical stories by our ancestors." Jason looks in the direction of the shapes that are formed in the sky.

"Turn around and face the North. Look, there you see the Polar Star. That is the point in heaven that appears to be the axis of the movement of the entire Universe. Our ancestors compared the journey of the stars with a river; they called it the Winding Waterway. When you look from the earth in this direction, all the lights appear to move into the direction of the Polar Star. They considered it to be a procession of spirits. Think of this Jason; high in the heavens they saw angels and gods, they were all on their way to the most sacred place in the heaven. To get there, these beings journeyed in large ships over the Cosmic Ocean."

"The constellations in the heaven are pictures designed in Antiquity. They are visible symbols that give access to the highest spiritual truths. This wisdom is literally written in the stars. This is the place that is called the 'Astral Realm'; Astra means star. The Astral World is the dimension of the archetypical stories connected to the stars. Every culture added their own stories. These stories tell about the difficult problems our ancestors were facing. In a way you can say that these stories describe ancient old patterns of human behavior."

"The Heaven and it's so called 'Astral Images' together form a 'Book of Wisdom.' A place wherein the highest wisdom and the most profound philosophical ideas have been kept safe; here the adventures of the Gods are written in the Stars."

I point towards a constellation that now rises above the horizon: "Do you see that row of three stars with the four stars surrounding it? That is the constellation Orion. It is connected to the story of the mythological hero. His name was Gilgamesh, Osiris, Hercules, Arthur, as well as many other names in the past." I look at Jason.

"What was the experience of this afternoon about?" he asks.

"What you saw was an appearance from the Astral World, the layer of consciousness that we are talking about right now." I point into the direction of the sea.

"Where the sun sinks, there is the West. The West is the entrance to the Otherworld. Through the Fisherking you get into contact with the Wisdom of the Stars, and you get directions for your personal path in life. They come forth immediately from your soul spark, your individual spiritual blueprint. You also get information about how you are connected to the world axis. We are all connected through this Axis Mundi.

"What do you choose, where do you focus on? When you focus on the other, on love and sharing, then you will experience connectedness. That is not in accordance with the Spirit of the Time of today. The mainstream culture is focused on competition, jealousy, egocentricity, and lust. Thus people become addicted to the energy of their survival instincts. They hunt after the same type of satisfaction as animals of prey. But people also have a deep need to connect. When you concentrate on that, you touch on the light side. Energy follows thought, and when you make that connection you will also attract unifying experiences. Jason, we need people who live this. People who want to train themselves to become channels for the forces of peace and goodness. Reality is formed by intention and focus, on the personal level, as well as on the level of groups and nations. Meanwhile the reality is endless, as endless as this ocean. When we build on a relation with this timeless eternity we become one with the cosmos."

I take Jason by his arm and together we stare in the direction of the endless sea. I hear how he sighs deeply, while he undergoes the healing experience of the landscape.

"Look, the moon is rising, she is full. Do notice that the tides are turning. It will now become flood." Together we walk along the edge of foam that decorates the coast with a collar of white lace. I point towards the shore: "Sea foam, the Goddess has started her creation."

Flood

From behind her Veils
Tethys waters her gardens,
From the foam she weaves Her robes.
While it contracts into solid matter,
Her face remains calm and serene.

The Water Spells

I contact the sea, I sniff her salty air, and admire her beautiful collar of sea foam. My heart goes out to the Moon who radiates her beauty above the ocean. I am aware of the fact that the tide turned and has become flood. I know that this tide, the presence of the sea foam and exactly this phase of the moon, are extremely efficient to create a beautiful future. I instruct Jason to copy my behavior.

"Stand straddle-legged and become aware of the endless abundance of the sea. Open your heart and imagine how the refreshing waters stream inside. Realize how the experiences and feelings from your heart want to melt together with those of our collective human consciousness; they flow back into the sea. Ebb and flood, reflection and expression, joy and sorrow: like it always was, it will always be. Look, Jason, do you see this path of light? Over this road we will call up the Watergod, his name is Hapi:"

> *I call upon the ancient Gods, the Gods from before the Flood[vii]*
> *Open, Winding Waterway, give access to the Magi!*
> *O Hapi, Watergod, come towards us over the Path of Light,*
> *Teach us Mastership over Water!*
>
> *O Moon-Eye, crying over the faith of the God Osiris:*
> *Grant that water to Hapi:*
> *Hapi, Watergod, refresh my heart and heal me with rushing water.*

The sea reacts instantly, the waves get higher. I point out to Jason how the clouds around the Moon start to whirl. They take on all kinds of shapes and an entity becomes visible in the mists. Around us, a slow drizzle starts to fall. "Listen to the sounds of the sea, Jason. Listen whether you can hear Hapi's voice:"

> *My name is Hapi, the Watergod.*
> *Invisible I travel through the primordial waters.*
> *Like a rushing river I traverse the Otherworld.*
> *As Winding Waterway, I water the fields in the Land of the Sun.*
> *I shed my tears to acknowledge the sorrow and honor the death.*
>
> *I poor myself out as life-giving water, a gift to all living beings.*
> *I open the Gates of the Flood:*
> *As Water from Heaven I descend to this Sacred Place.*

Then it starts to rain … and what makes it extra special is that the Moon remains visible. "Jason, it is important that you make an image, an i-magi-nation of what you desire, because Hapi gives form to the images you carry in your heart."

Then I vibrate the next Water Spell over the ocean. While I do that, I create visions of harmony, of love and healing. I visualize how Jason's heart heals and how he heals himself in a sunlit landscape. I imagine how the water purifies the heart. I am very precise in my images and support, without interfering or meddling, the healing that Jason wishes for himself:

Oh Hapi, great in the Heavens, the Heavens are safe.
I ask you: Give us Mastership over Water,
Like the Goddess Sekhmet who saved Osiris in the Night of the Storm.

Behold, the Gods create abundance:
They have made me to sail the Winding Waterway!
When the Winds blow from the North, I will set sail to the South.
When the Winds blow from the South, I will journey to the West.
I breathe in the Winds
And sail towards the place where I long to be.[viii]

Together we stand at the seashore, amidst of the wind, the rain, the waves, with our feet in the foam. "Do you feel the water, Jason? The sea now flows as ebb and flood in your heart. With ebb it takes the dead impulses with it and thus it creates space for new experiences. At flood it brings a wave of new adventures and possibilities. That is the rhythm of the Moon that is the eternal dance of the tides of the sea. This is how it ever was, and this is how it will always be."

A voice calls from the distance, I hear my name. I turn around and see Eagle and Gabriella walking towards us. They wave. Jason and I walk in their direction. I greet both of them.
"What a beautiful large full moon," Eagle says.
"A fantastic environment for Water Spells," Gabriella answers.
"You are never allowed to guess again," I smile.
I introduce Jason to Gabriella. Gabriella is a warm-hearted woman of 38 years old, a little bit older than Jason. She has long brown hair and green eyes. With her tall posture she is a beauty to see. Gabriella made her entrance years ago into the group. Slowly she got accustomed with the work, and her psychic talents have developed so strongly that she became a part of my team.
"It is time to leave the beach and search for a dry spot," Eagle says. "You have been busy so long that I thought it was time to check out."
"You have sensed us perfectly," I say to Gabriella and Eagle.
And we decide to finish the evening in the beach house, where now all the lights are burning. The light of the lighthouse splits the darkness of the evening. I observe it and make a connection to this beacon of light and the Watchtower of the West. In myself, in silence I resonate the adoration for the Watchtower of the West:

Thank you, Royal star Antares, Cosmic Eagle
Thank you, Lord of Spirit
Who exchanges the messages between gods and humans.

Back at the beach house we order a drink and enter into an interesting discussion. It is nice that Jason learns to know some of the others in such an informal way. The conversation is about the meaning of life, and the solutions for the problems of the planet pass within half an hour. Eagle is talkative. He underlines his arguments with broad arm gestures. His voice rises and his eyes sparkle, while he declares emotionally: "The great drama of the modern world is the tarnishing of religion. Throughout the centuries the churches played a political game and have corrupted themselves. Thus, they caused rejection in our time and are responsible for the aversion of great groups for spiritual richness."

Jason answers: "But those classical religious ideas have become outdated, they no longer fit to our modern society."

Gabriella smiles and answers: "You need to divide between religion as an institution and the transpersonal experience. These are two different things. A religion is meant to offer a moral compass to the masses. To give them direction by means of values, norms, and dogma's. That does not necessary entail inner work or insight. Transpersonal development leads to individuation and asks for reflection, for the internalization of a certain cultural inheritance. It also aims at causing existential experiences that result in an expansion of consciousness."

Jason thinks whether this philosophy would make an article. *Would there be a market for this type of knowledge?*

Eagle elaborates on Gabriella's words: "By generating transpersonal peak experiences, you strengthen the essence of your being. Everyone going through this path of self-development learns to translate his insights to his life and work. This causes a wave of spiritual consciousness to flow into society, to the working space, to families. The question about the deeper meaning is the ancient old quest for the Grail."

"What is the Grail?" Jason asks. "Is it happiness?"

"I went through a burnout," Eagle answers. "I needed to make a plan for my boss for the energy production. I got trapped in an ethical split. What to do; continue to write articles and develop technology on behalf of the propaganda machine, whose only goal is to make the people swallow a policy that is not of their interest? Then you become a partner in crime! I became trapped in an impossible dilemma. I want to serve society with my work, to contribute to finding healthy sustainable solutions for problems. But that was not the direction that my boss wanted to go. Always you are told that it is about earning back an investment with the highest possible profit. But do you know what the real goal is? That remote country that cashes the profit makes a bit for the power over the world! I worked there and I was asked to collect the scientific arguments to help to establish a world vision that is not mine. The exploitation of energy resources brings money and generates an infrastructure to establish a world power that is based on a different and rigid world philosophy. That is the real goal!

"What to do when you are in a position where you are payed to justify ideas that are not yours? I have consulted my soul, and my only option was to return the mission because I did not find another solution to this wicked dilemma. Do you work towards your own goals or do you surrender to the dominance of others? I have changed jobs and now use my talent to develop different plans. In the end it comes down to the fact that we need to educate society and ask the population whether we are allowed to make money in such a way! There are people who, like the God Prometheus, steal fire from heaven!"

Jason is silent. Memories awaken. 'There are people who are convinced that they can exploit nature to its utter limits, to reach their individual goals," he answers. "The greater their power, the bigger the destruction, the more ruthless their methods of operating, it seems."

His thoughts go back a few years in time when he was driving through Naples for his work. He saw a gigantic wood fire. Helicopters and firemen were working night and day to extinguish the fires. To his amazement, he saw that from the ground the helicopters were shot at. Because he was so shocked about the scene, he investigated it and discovered that the fires had been ignited by the Mob. They had found a hole in the law; when the woods would cease to exist as a protected nature area, the ground could be used to build expensive offices. *There are forces that use our valuable nature as a paper towel, blow your nose in it, and throw it away...*

I add my viewpoint to the conversation: "That is why it is extra important that professionals open themselves and develop extra sensibility in a stable way, open themselves for the spiritual reality. When that stability is not anchored, your pilgrimage becomes a flight to Lala-land: the realm of dreamers who escape from the world. It is of the utmost importance to teach professionals a method by which they can fine-tune their inner compass on their mission in life and the interests of the collective. With the disappearance of the determination of value through religious dogma's the individuation process of professionals has become of vital importance."

"What do you mean by the individuation process?" Jason asks. "Wasn't that an invention of Jung?"

"No, it was not invented by Jung," I answer. "Jung was important, because he translated the ancient Hermetic Mysteries into science. He followed the footsteps of others. Among them were great names like Mozart, Paracelcus, Nostradamus, Newton, and many important artists, noblemen, priests, and scientists. The chain goes back into the distant past. The individuation process connects people with the transpersonal."

"What exactly is the transpersonal?" Jason asks.

"It is the Collective Super Consciousness. It consists of ancient old patterns of behavior that generate development and growth. It is anchored in a language of images, which you also find within religious symbolism.

"When people get connected to the transpersonal, they become anchored in their ethical core. This inner work makes them autonomous and congruent. It connects people with their mission in life; they become as stable as a house and get less vulnerable to manipulation from outside."

"That all sounds very nice," Jason answers. "The arena of every day floods you with stress and conflicting interests. How to protect your autonomy in that warzone? How to stay in contact with your soul?"

Gabriella bends forward and looks Jason in the eyes. "The reflection on the spiritual dimension always provides me with a deeper perspective on the cause of the crises and the challenges in my life. It always works to observe my life from a more abstract and higher level. I have been spiritual all my life, but I was unable to hold on to the higher experiences that I had. I know very well that not everyone has these experiences. How to make sure that you don't give up? Because of my high sensitivity, I am so transparent that I constantly absorb the chaos around me. Some very nasty things happened to me in the past because of this. That is why I closed down everything. But that does not work in the long term. At a certain moment the water breaks through the dykes and you become flooded, a flood of images from another world. It also doesn't help to solve mundane problems. You need to connect both worlds!"

Jason holds his breath. Gabrielle describes her own experiences. That is what is happening to him right now. "How did you solve this?" he asks. The question comes from the bottom of his heart; he realizes that the water has risen to his lips.

Gabriella answers: "I have gained a lot by the training and the fact that I belong to a group of likeminded people. Within an order or another community, it is much easier to live hand-in-hand with your soul. I get insights and breakthroughs, mostly in dreams. But I never learned to trust my intuition, or on images, or unheard realizations in my mind. Because of my training I hear magical spells sing in the background of my mind. I see this as extremely reassuring because I know that my soul keeps in contact with the goals I have set for myself. And when I get into a crisis, they hold me on the right track. They protect me."

Jason listens intently. Melusine nods to Gabriella in a gesture of assurance. "You have formulated that beautifully, Gabriella. It is about those deeper insights that break through suddenly and give a new perspective. They are granted to you, but on top of that you can train your mind to open to this inspiration, so that it becomes a reliable source of information. Let me explain the effect of the symbolic images. They work like a search engine for the brain, to dig through the subconscious mind; they can trigger deep insights."

Gabriella's eyes start to shine. "That is new information for me; I will pay attention to that. Very interesting! I always became angry because I did not understand them. Also, when something was said to me from the spiritual world, I find it difficult to interpret. Meanwhile, I know that I need to accept it and brood over it until I understand it."

I smile and bend over to Gabriella. Softly I touch her arm and confide: "These images and that internal communication are extremely important. When you train to receive them, the fragments develop into a deep communication. I always joke that it is essential to first learn the language of the imaginative; it is the language of the subconscious mind. When you don't know the language, it remains unconscious, instead developing into a consciousness of the 'under-world.'

Jason nods enthusiastically, as a token of recognition. Then he asks: "But how do you do that? What I see around me is that many spiritual people are living in a fantasy world, but all of you seem to be very sober and down to earth. What is the difference?"

Gabriella leans forward and answers: "We follow a path that has been followed throughout the ages. It is called the 'Hermetic Mystery Tradition,' and goes back all the way down into antiquity. This has always been the path that the intellectuals, the scientists, nobility, and the priesthood went. When you know where to pay attention, you will discover that every generation left an extensive curriculum of literature for the future generations. The Hermetic Mystery Tradition is not a religion but a lifestyle, a philosophy, a school a choice for self-realization, gained by an intensive training. It is very spiritual and generates life changing peak experiences."

Eagle ads: "Practicing mental techniques at random, mixing beginners stuff and advanced material, mixing techniques from different traditions at random is a risky business. You run the risk of dissociation, emotions, observations, and memories are no longer connected. There is the risk of ego-inflation: people get the idea that they are the reincarnation of important spiritual examples and start to behave in such a way. Compare transpersonal development with walking on a path through the woods. You need to stay on the path; otherwise you run the risk of losing your way."

"That sounds dangerous," Jason remarks.

"No, it is stubborn and stupid to try to find a way on your own through a jungle, because that path is the result of the experiences of the generations of people who walked before us through those woods."

Then I add: "From the beginning of civilization the Mages and the Mystics have put signposts beside the road. The most important signpost is neglected most often. That is the one that indicates that this is the 'Golden Path;' you follow the Light while you travel. You follow the Path of the Sun."

Jason is confused; "What does that mean, following the Path of the Sun?"

I answer. "That means that you are guided by the Light at all times, the Light of Higher Consciousness. You follow that light. There are many people who don't get this. They think that they need to defeat their personal demons in the darkness. They descend into the underworld and get lost in that utterly dangerous world of phantoms. The results of that misunderstanding are, for example, depressions or addictions. Or when the increasing energy ends up in a kundalini-crisis, when awakening goes into a skid and ends up in a psychosis. When you travel the Path of the Sun, you also traverse the subconscious areas. That can only be done without risk when you are being led by your Higher-Self. Then you can actually see what you are facing, name it, and transform it. How to do that, I will explain to you later."

Then Eagle takes back the stage. He speaks with a lot of passion: "It is important to make people conscious of the fact that there are proven systems for people to develop. To get access to the resources for everyone, and meanwhile respect the life on this planet. A conscious culture of love, compassion, and tolerance between us is vital. On top of that there needs to be respect and consciousness about the unity. Respect for the life on earth and awe for the forces that are bigger than us."

Jason is genuinely interested now. Wondering, he takes in the body of thought that is completely new to him. "How does one accomplish that?"

"The Golden Path is a training, an education," I answer. "By training the mind (in the right sequence), the effects of the exercises start to accumulate. You improve your personal effectiveness, grow spiritually, and your inner senses develop, so that you slowly grow into mediumship and become a channel between this world and the Otherworld. You learn to combine the daily reality and the extra-sensual reality and develop into a Walker-between-the-Worlds. You learn to work with magical energy. The first and most important step is to learn to control your emotions; to learn to feel more deep and accurate, to sharpen your intuition. That is what we call "Control over Water," finally you learn to "Walk on Water.' Then you contact the Otherworld and are able to generate spiritual experiences at will. This assures you of living an inspired life and enables you to generate the material effects that you need to continue your mission. Your spiritual work will translate itself into your job and your relationships. By means of the Hermetic training you get access to the spiritual realm. You will benefit from the experiences of your fellow travelers and of former generations. You are being helped to avoid the pitfalls, and within a Hermetic School the trainers know exactly in what stage of your spiritual development you are in and what area you can most profitably set your next steps."

Jason listens breathlessly. "I had no idea that something like this existed. Can anyone follow this training?"

The Ship of Stars

"Yes, everyone who is willing to do the work and who wants to set foot on the path from the beginning. Only then you lay down the solid foundations where upon the effects of the magical exercises can be build. The spiritual exercises will assure that you stay rooted and will have a healing effect on your hormonal system and your neurological system. That will result in a balanced sensitivity, immunity to stress, and increasing extra sensitive experiences that will feed your soul. Within the context of a well-managed spiritual school your social life will improve. Hermetic institutes underline that the real work needs to be done in your own life. A magical training must never be a flight!"

"I love your name, Jason!" Gabriella remarks. "It reminds me of the story of Jason and the Argonauts."
"I don't know that story. What is it about?" Jason looks around him to see who will inform him about the answer. Melusine starts to talk. "That is a very apt story. We can go out for a few minutes, enjoy the night and travel for a short while on the meditation of the Ship of Stars. Then I will return home urgently, it is getting late."
The companions leave the beach house and walk over the wooden planking to the loose sand. There they sit down, watching the endless vastness; they let themselves be carried by the sounds of the waves and Melusine's hypnotic voice:

"Listen to the rushing sound of the sea, and look ahead to the boundless distances ahead. Endless velvet deep stretches out in front of you. You realize that you are at the beginning of a great adventure. Feel the atmosphere of expectation that is tangible at the border 'Between the Worlds.' The night is adorned with twinkling stars. Travel with me in your imagination. Follow me into that world where the Wisdom of the Stars is stored. In the cosmos a vast amount of wisdom has been left behind for us by our ancestors. It contains the eternal Knowledge of the Gods, of nature, and of the human heart. Follow me on this road.

"Here time does not exist, there are no boundaries. The path is safe. In front of you, you see an illuminated square; it is the 'Door-between-the-Worlds.' Follow me through this door. I take a handful of stardust from the bucket at my belt and throw it into the air. The twinkling glitter reveals an invisible staircase. In our mind we climb the stairs. While we climb the Stairway to Heaven, we become aware of the star clusters, looming up on our left and right side. They are charged with intelligence. One by one they are Worlds of Light. Look straight ahead of you in the South, there is a harbor. It is called Lapis Lazuli Harbor. This is the place where the ship of the gods docks at the shore of the Earth. In antiquity this ship was world famous. In Egypt it was called the 'Boat of Millions of Years.' In Greece they called it the Argo. Look in the distance; you see the ship sailing towards us. The sail of the ship is deep blue and adorned with golden stars.

"Watch how the ship approaches the shore and anchors. On the prow people are waiting in Greek clothing. Leading the way is a remarkable character. He is dressed in a panther skin. The man steps forward and has his arms crossed over his chest. He has clear blue eyes and looks directly at us. *My name is Jason,* he says. *I am on a mission. I need a crew of mortal humans to row the fifty oars of my boat. Follow me!* Jason walks to the prow of the ship and rubs the figurehead with a dot of sheep wool that he has hidden somewhere underneath his cloths. To our amazement the wood starts to talk. First we hear the sounds of trumpets coming from all the Four Corners of the Cosmos. The sound echoes back, and to our amazement, we hear a voice:"

Listen to the sounds of the trumpets of the Heavenly Boat!
I call upon the bravest warriors.
Warriors of the World, come to me and join me on an adventure.

"When Jason sees our asking faces he points at the figure head and says: *This was a gift of the Goddess Athens. She took a piece of the Talking Oak of Dodona and made a figure head from it. It only guides those who want to listen to its voice.* From all the corners of the heavens they come; they march in long rows. All the heroes from Antiquity come to the ship, by foot, by horse, by car, by tank, and by plane. There is one woman standing at the shore. She really wants to join but cannot step aboard. Jason then takes off one sandal and puts it on his head. He sets his bare foot in the water, lifts the woman and carries her aboard the ship. When both his feet are back on the ship, it is shows that he has been bitten in his heel, probably by an animal that was hidden under the surface of the water."

"Jason speaks again: 'Let us hurry, because we have work to do. Our job is to search for the Golden Fleece and return it to the Earth. Jason answers the question that forms in our minds. What is the Golden Fleece?

That is the Light that falls over creation. It is the Light that makes everything visible to humans and Gods. It is made from the Breath of the Sea God Poseidon, when he fell in love with the Goddess of the Divine Voice. It is the in- and outbreath of Divinity in the form of Light. It is the Breath of Light that grows in intensity during the seasons until midsummer, and then it slowly colors the landscape in the shades of autumn, and cools down at the end of the year. Then, during the three days of the Winter solstice it withdraws in its core. The Golden Fleece is a priceless treasure. It is the key to the door that connect the world of humanity with the Divine. You can observe it everywhere around you, but it is only visible for those who know the secret and are capable of looking with the Eyes of Truth. Take this knowledge with you; store it in your heart. All of you belong to the treasure keepers of the Golden Fleece and when you meet this ship again on your journey, an even greater secret will be revealed to you. But for now it is time to leave this Ship of Stars and return to your own reality.

"One by one we leave the boat and when everyone is back on the beach of Lapis Lazuli Harbor, Jason turns around and asks the men at the oars to turn the ship. From the shore we watch how this mighty Ship of Stars sails away and returns to the Ocean Between the Worlds. We descend the Stairway to Heaven and return in our own tempo to the World of Time where our physical bodies rest. Return to the here and now, and open your eyes."

I observe how everyone gently returns from the meditation and I rise. I clean my clothes from the sand and uselessly try to comb my blown about hair back into shape with my fingers.

Everyone is now standing and strolling around after the deep trance. Then we walk back over the wooden footboards. I look at my mobile, worry a bit about the time. It has become very late. Time to go back. "Jason, where is your car?"

With a little bit of head-breaking we solve the transport problem. Eagle will drive me home and Jason takes Gabriella.

We say our goodbyes. I take Jason's hands and look him in the eyes: "It will improve from now on, I am convinced of that. I think that it is important that you wear your ring tonight during your sleep. Try to remember your dream and write it down as detailed as possible. Email it to me tomorrow."

Jason reacts reserved: "I need to think this through and let it sink in." I nod and smile, then we say goodbye.

*****

Back home Jason reflects on a turbulent day. How to continue his life? What is the meaning of the strange illuminated guide? Then he picks up the box of bone. He sighs. He takes out the magical ring from the box and wonders what exactly is the influence of this ring on the events. Melusine suggested wearing it tonight. Is that sensible to do, knowing the effect that this piece of jewelry has on him? He looks at the signs. The eye in the ring radiates six rays that seem to get more intense. Without thinking the ring finds his finger. He takes a notebook and a pen, and puts them aside of his bed. Then he falls into a deep and quiet sleep.

Suddenly he finds himself in front of the Double Doors, and the Guardian approaches him. He asks: "Why did you come to this place?"
I come to learn to get control over Water.
The double doors open and he enters into a strange space. The floor is paved with black and white tiles. In the middle stands a cubical shaped altar, where upon lies a baby made of clay. Jason looks around, confused. *Where is this place?* He sees the large pillars. While he stands at the altar, to his amazement four shining beings appear.
The first entity steps forward, ignites a torch and upholds it. Then words echo, or are they ideas that form in his mind? Jason listens intensively and feels how his heart starts to beat. He feels an emptiness in his heart that longs to be filled, a yearning, an intensive need to let himself flow into this magical atmosphere and connect himself with it:

I illuminate my torch to serve the Light,
To empower the Winged Human
That lives within the depths of the soul of our species:
Guide us through our sacred transformations,
Learn us how to shapeshift, to use our animal powers ethically;
That makes people change into eagles, into deer and wolves.

> *Let me learn from your wisdom:*
> *I kneel and surrender to your guidance.*

Then the second figure steps forward and kneels at the altar. Jason feels embarrassed. Did he arrive at the wrong place? Does he have a right to be here? Meanwhile, he is fascinated by what he sees and hears. The words of the two lightning beings echo through the space:

> *I illuminate my torch to serve the Light,*
> *To empower the Winged Human Being*
> *That lives within the heart of our species:*
> *Teach us how to walk under Water or on Water.*
> *Guide our spirits through the Astral Seas*
> *Lead us to that Great Temple in the Cosmic Ocean:*
> *I kneel and surrender to your guidance.*

The third entity steps forward, also igniting a torch.

> *I illuminate my torch to serve the Light,*
> *To empower the Winged Human Being*
> *That lives within the heart of our species:*
> *Bring me sacred visions,*
> *Teach me to speak the language of lakes and rivers,*
> *Of flowers and meadows, of trees and of woods,*
> *Teach me to listen to your voice,*
> *I kneel and surrender to your guidance.*

The fourth entity completes the pattern. Jason is now surrounded by four lightning entities. He wants to step aside and make space, but to his amazement he notices that he walks through the altar. He tests it, reaches forward to the objects at the altar, but his hand grasps into thin air. The fourth figure speaks now:

> *I illuminate my torch to serve the Light*
> *To empower the Winged Human Being*
> *That lives within the heart of our species:*
>
> *Teach me how to cure all illnesses,*
> *Teach me the art to make a Temple from my body.*
> *Teach me to penetrate every cell of my body and cure it.*
> *I kneel and surrender to your guidance.*

The four entities step forward again, as if they don't see him. One even walks right through him. The four bring their torches together above the altar, so that the four flames melt together into one. Then they bring the flame downward to the clay baby. Suddenly, Jason's perspective changes completely. His voice formulates strange words, they echo through the hall:

> *Let's play this crazy game on the Chessboard of Life,*
> *That dance between joy and sorrow;*
> *And journey from Time to Eternity.*

It is as if he is pulled into the clay and suddenly he perceives the temple from the eyes of the clay figure. He witnesses how the shining entities stand above him and he looks them in the eyes. He hears the words; *He awakens,* and sits upright. Completely stunned he looks around him. The lights in the temple start to shine, change shape, and become constellations. Above his head he clearly sees a rose with all kinds of symbols inside, which he now recognizes as Hebrew letters. Seven energy orbs float through the space. Flabbergasted, he anchors the images. The words of Melusine rise up from his memory: *Try to remember the dream as detailed as possible and note it down.*

Then he shoots upright and wakes up. He grabs his notebook and pen and starts to write down his experiences.

*****

The Dragons under the Mountain

5

THE DRAGONS UNDER THE MOUNTAIN

Everything of Value is Vulnerable[ix]

Quickly Jason walks through the front door of his publisher. Behind the desk sits Elly, the receptionist, she is having her lunch break. While she eats her bread, she is in an intensive conversation with Jeanette, the girl of the administration department. Two beautiful faces adorned by silver jewelry, bow over a spiritual magazine. On the open pages Jason sees an illustration of a unicorn, decorated by a rainbow. He catches bits and pieces of the conversation as they talk about the efficiency of the gemstones that Elly put down in the bedroom of her son.

"He really starts to sleep much better since I put that rose quarts at his window", Elly says. Jeanette answers that it can also help to sprinkle some lavender around. "It works really great when such a small child has difficulties cooling down." Together they flip through the pages of the magazine, while they chit-chat and exchange all kinds of spiritual tips and tricks for everyday problems.

Jason's neck hair rises; this is exactly what he is allergic to. This gives him the feeling that there is no structure in that spiritual world. The lame are helping the blind with placebos, and the only ones benefitting are the dealers in 'cuddling stones'.

In his mind he hears the cynical laughter of his colleagues, the condescending remarks about the non-scientific quality of alternative therapies. He feels his resistance against quackery rising from his stomach by the minute. He approaches the girls and asks them straight forward whether the ladies also consult tarot readers, or the soothsayers from the spiritual television stations? And whether they follow their advice?

Elly and Jeanette look up surprised from their magazine. Elly draws in a breath, swallows her bread, and quickly thinks of an answer. "It is not only in the head, Mister Adams." She points to her chest and says; "Some things you can only feel, deep inside."

Jeannette nods and adds: "You feel at the energy whether it is good or not, and then you do something about it. A medium feels things in a different way, and gets answers from a perspective that you wouldn't access in the normal way." They look at Jason pitying, as if he is the one who lives in an alien world.

Jason sighs; *apparently, living in this manner fulfills an important part in their lives, but I do not understand it at all.*

Jason's mobile rings, it's his friend Tom. Tom nowadays lives in Bretagne. He has been Jason's sports comrade for years. Half a year ago Tom moved to Vannes and is now employed in the Breton tourist industry.

It would be really nice to have a chat with that chap, Jason thinks, so he takes some time to answer the call.

Enthusiastically, Tom informs Jason about his work and his whereabouts in Bretagne. He tells of the extensive possibilities to sport, the biking routes, and the track along the rocky shores with amazing views. He informs him about the possibilities to sail before the Breton coast, and of course about the fabulous nightlife in the tourist villages.

"Hey, man, this paradise over here! I absolutely do not regret taking this step and moving over."

They talk about their jobs and Jason tells Tom about the project he recently started.

"A medical conference in Florence. Visited the city, isn't that old-fashioned? Ah... you found it interesting? Astonishing that someone wants to study this stuff in this time and age. What did Joan think about it, did she like it?"

Jason quickly diverts the conversation into another direction. "Business journey, not compatible with girls. You need to do things for yourself within a relation." And he distracts Tom by naming the figures involved in the project. Tom is complete and utterly impressed.

Then Tom switches to the subject that is the real reason for his call: "I have developed a new program, namely a sport weekend for men. How do you feel about coming to Vannes shortly to be my guinea pig? All those entrepreneur gatherings, required dinners and parties, must make it necessary for you to work out regularly. I have put together an excellent program; when you come over for a weekend you will conquer that beer belly of yours." Tom exclaims enthusiastically.

Jason watches his waistband, no sign of love handles there. He squeezes the skin above his hips and concludes that he can always improve it.

"Maintain that six-pack, come over to convalescent! Start a frontal attack against all the lazy sweat and sitting fat. When you return, you will be a jaguar in top condition. I have defined a biking track which includes some challenging slopes. The ground is so uneven that it beats every cardio program of your sports school. The view is even better, because we will drive along the rock formations at the shore. Work yourself to the bone against the elements. Your metabolism will speed up and you will burn a lot of fat. In the evening you choose from the special healthy meals without feeling guilty. You will conquer your belly with those superfoods, like those top managers. They are indispensable when you train your muscles. For the evenings I have a cool program in case you want to enjoy the nightlife. Before you know your outside equals your inside again and do you win the battle against your inertia beast. After such a weekend you belong again to that easy inflammable type that can perform."

Jason is attracted by the idea, it could be a great distraction and he wants to visit Bretagne anyway. Not only for Tom and the sport, but also because of some historical places he wants to visit. The appointment is quickly made and it is not difficult under these circumstances to find a weekend that he is free to go. Bretagne is just a few hours away with the car. When he hits the gas he will be there in no time. They compare their schedules and find out that the coming weekend would fit both. Why wait?

At the end of Friday afternoon Jason arrives in Vannes. From a far distance he sees the banner with the weapon of the city flying on the wind. Admiring, he looks around: it is a beautiful mediaeval town. Slowly he drives his car through the center until he reaches the city wall, where the pedestrian area starts. Most certainly a place where he would want to drink a beer later on. But first he searches for Toms place to settle and unpack his suitcase.

Tom lives outside of the city walls. He greets Jason warmheartedly. "Hey, fellow, good to see you," he says as the two men shake hands and pat each other on the shoulders. After Jason has established himself and rested from the journey, they decide to visit the town. Tom is very enthusiastic and eager to show why he chose this environment. They park the car outside of the city walls and walk to the center. Jason looks around and his interest for historical places is awakened immediately. The town has a complete mediaeval center and is surrounded by a massive old city wall.

He admires the timber framing of the houses. They have four floors and every floor is a bit larger than the one underneath. The overhang is supported by beautiful heavy wooden carriers. The facades are all extraordinary pieces of mediaeval craftsmanship.

The shops are framed with beautiful woodcutting. The church towers distinctive above the houses; the spire reaching for heaven and is surrounded by four smaller spires. The woodwork of the houses has been painted in different earth colors and the masonry is plastered. The roofs are covered with grey schist and the windows are decorated with colorful flower pots. Everything is gorgeous and stylish.

The city wall encircles the town; they provide an atmosphere of security, a feeling of protection and cheerfulness. At the corner of the street, musicians enhance the atmosphere with French Celtic music. Billboards decorate the facades with gracious old-fashioned letters. They are decorated with beautiful mediaeval paintings. Over the doors, sculptures illustrate what professions were active in the old houses. Outside of the city wall, dignified gardens have been constructed. Jason and Tom walk further and they arrive at a small harbor, wherein boats for pleasure cruising float. At the edge of the city center there are convivial terraces. Jason and Tom decide to have a seat there.

They choose a café called 'Auster', southern wind. It has a billboard that depicts a knight carrying shield and sword. On the shield is a picture of the sun.

Tom tells Jason enthusiastically about the local stories telling about King Arthur. According to those stories he would have won a battle over here against the Visigoths. The environment also holds some magical stories. Merlin the Mage would have been buried nearby in a wood called Brocéliande. There are stories about a fairy queen called Melusine ... *Melusine, what a coincidence that this name pops up here. I definitely need to dig up more information about that name. For some reason it triggers me,* Jason thinks.

The district has a very rich history. And when he searches for mediaeval inspiration he most certainly needs to visit the castle and the lake amidst of Brocéliande; and of course pay a visit to the grave of Merlin, nearby at Paimpoint.

Then Tom explains what kind of program he has for Jason and they discuss the details of their shared activities, with the exception of Sunday morning, when Tom has an appointment that he cannot change connected to the sailing program he wants to develop for his series of events.

"No problem," Jason says, "that will be my time to visit the chateau. After that we can have lunch before I drive home."

Jason leaves the town on his bike, heads for the Breton countryside with the map on his steering wheel, his bidon filled with sport drink, and energy bars in the pockets on his back. The road bends and enters into a wood. The atmosphere is charged: the sunlight flickers through the branches and golden rays penetrate a foggy atmosphere. The wood changes into a play of colors of a golden green beauty. He paddles through woods filled with fir and mossy cobbles. *There is something about this landscape,* Jason thinks without being able to define what that 'something' could be. *It is mysterious and raises my neck hair. The trees have such whimsical shapes that they resemble mythical creatures.*

Suddenly, the trees give way and Jason is at a dirt road. It is still possible to drive here, so he paddles on, carefully steering around the cobbles and the pot holes to avoid getting a flat tire.

He paddles along a meadow. In the middle stands a lonely well. The well is made of large stones and a rusty pulley hangs lifeless under the shelter.

Suddenly, buildings loom up from the mist. He looks at his map and sees that he is at Chateau de Comper. Large round castle towers arise above the leaf canopy. A green sign made for tourists offers an explanation:

"According to the Celtic legends this castle is the birthplace of Viviane Lefay. She was a water nymph and was called the Lady of the Lake in the Arthurian legends.

In the lake behind the castle, named Lac Diane, Viviane's Crystal Palace would be hidden under the water."

Jason takes a closer look at the intriguing hewn archway and window openings. He studies the architecture of the building. The walls look unstable at places, like they are on the point of collapsing. They carry the scars of the times. They are battered and full with long cracks. You can look right through the cleaves at some places.

Jason puts his bike against a wall. The castle is surrounded by a strange silence. The atmosphere is foggy; the stones are weathered, colored black by the moisture and overgrown by green mosses. The passing clouds overhead are about to spill their wet content at any minute. In the grey clouds, heads appear and Jason is aware of a growing tension in his lower belly. The wet, moist atmosphere feels depressing, almost sad. Jason can imagine the former glory of the place, but now the atmosphere is ghastly, charged by neglect and decay. The lake next to the castle doesn't make it any better. It looks sinister: dead trees rise from the waters, gleaming from moist. Their bare branches point upwards to the grey heaven, as if they are raising their arms in despair.

Jason walks to the tower and looks upward into a space without ceilings. An empty shaft with holes instead of windows, and openings where once would have been doors. He can clearly see where the ceiling carriers once supported the wooden floors. He walks further around the building, searching for a staircase. He would like to climb the tower and indeed; after a while he finds an old spiral shaped staircase, hewn from rough stones. The stairs look intact so Jason climbs upwards and passes empty rooms. He can almost reach the top of the tower.

When he is upstairs he overlooks the landscape; it is a fantastic view! He imagines what the castle would have looked like in its glory days. Probably there were archers on the archway. He imagines how the knights came riding in on their horses, flanked by their pages, upholding their banners in the wind. In his mind he hears trumpeters blowing and sees how the guardians, clothed in chainmail, protected the building. They would probably blow their trumpets as a warning in case they would see unknown folk approaching the castle. In his mind he hears the rattling noise of the chains of the drawbridge and the sound of horses. He sniffs the air, and smells the stables and the smoking fires. He hears the sound of metal, and in his imagination large cooking kettles hang above the fires and he smells the scents of the preparation of food.

Jason investigates the ruins of the castle until he knows every corner. Then he walks into the woods. At the border of the lake a lonely heron stares in the water on one leg. Between the bushes appears a narrow path. Jason is curious where it will bring him. He follows the winding forest road and arrives at an empty space in the woods. Two standing stones appear to mark a passage; as an invisible gate they appear to give access to a circle of trees, marked by a ring of standing stones. In the middle of the stone circle stands a cleft menhir. On it are wild flowers that have been put there carefully. Jason walks into the open space. Again he feels touched by the light that like a golden shower shines through the leaves. Jason decides to walk towards the stones. They resemble an altar. He wipes away the moss from the main stone and sees an ancient old inscription, but the script is so weathered that he just barely can distinguish some letters:

MER..N

The rest is completely illegible. He just wants to turn around to continue, when an owl comes flying toward the menhir and lands on the top. The light suddenly changes in intensity and a figure appears in the shadows between the trees.

"Welcome, Jason," the entity speaks. "Welcome at the Fallen Stone. The laws of synchronicity work perfect! I have been waiting for you. What lives in you, mirrors itself in your life, and what is outside of you is a perfect reflection of yourself. Behold, do you see how this once so mighty menhir has been cleaved? This mighty stone has fallen. Just like Chateau de Comper became destroyed by the ravages of time. Do you want to know what caused the great tower of the castle to fall and who caused it? When you want to know, I will tell you; I will show it to you. Do you know what is beneath the tower of this castle? The lake passes along right underneath it. Beneath it is another building and a space filled with water. Under this pool of water, two dragons lie dormant. One dragon is red and the other one white. They are huge! They feel that the water becomes increasingly heavy and it pushes on their backs. They get restless and this makes the water in the pool burble. That causes so much turbulence that anything that is built on top, will inevitably collapse. Also, your tower collapses because of the dragons![x] Be alert and conscious, Jason, because the Tides are rough." And the figure begins to fade away again.

"Wait," Jason exclaims, "who are you, what is your name?"

And in the thin air an echo resounds: "My name is carved onto the altar stone."

Then the light disappears and Jason is left alone, within the woods, next to an old menhir.

The clouds gather and it becomes even darker. Jason takes his phone from his back pocket and makes some pictures of the stone trying to get a good image of the letters that are on it. Then he walks back to the castle, to the place where he parked his bike. He takes a few more photos of the chateau and then the rain starts to gush down. Quickly he pulls his raincoat on. *Time to drive back to Vannes,* he thinks. At the end of the cart track he can move faster, but he is already soaked. He turns his head around to have a last view of the castle, and to his amazement he sees a lightning flash hitting the highest tower. He decides not to tell Tom about his strange experiences. *He would not understand one word of it,* Jason thinks.

Back in Vannes the two men meet each other again. The heroes' sweat is washed off and the biking clothes exchanged for a tailor made suit. After the healthy sweating of a weekend workout to upgrade the body, it is now time to consume a firm serving of animal fat in one of the restaurants in the center of the town.

The men talk and Jason confesses his new status of bachelor and the discussions he had with Joan about becoming parents; "What if I would not like such a child, you cannot send them back once they are there!"

"What did Joan say?" Tom wants to know. "Nowadays, woman can make a nice career if they want?"

"She told me that she always wanted children. She said that she was tired of feeling the pain of missing them; a pain that became increasingly heavy to bear. She said she wants a real connection, with a man who respects the wish of his wife and find it self-evident."

"Ouch," Tom exclaims. "That is a real deal breaker man! I think that it is time for you to reconnect with the gang. It is better to be a part of a group of comrades than to be one half of a couple: that is also my motto. There is one advantage to this situation, boy, now you have time for a new hobby."

Then it is time to say goodbye. Jason needs some hours to drive back to the Netherlands. "We will keep in contact," he says to Tom. They give each other friendly pushes as a goodbye. Jason steps into his road tiger, turns the key, lets the sound of the motor swell, and tears off.

*****

Suddenly I become aware of the deeper message in my meditation. I feel in my mind from where the information is coming, that wants to reveal itself to me. My meditation changes in character. I hear the chiming of bells and a shining figure comes walking towards me. I follow him to the stone circle, located in the middle of a wood. The entity makes a ritual gesture and the open space changes into a tree cathedral. A gateway appears that gives access to the Otherworld. I bow to follow and enter.

The space is decorated very plain. One of the stones is engraved with a Celtic Cross, the characteristic motive is skillfully carved out of the natural stone. In the middle stands an altar stone. On it, two burning candles of beeswax. A small ray of sunlight falls in and illuminates the chapel. The shining figure points at the altar stone. He speaks to me: "Decipher the secret of Myrddin."

I look at him, questioning.

He shows me a vision of a castle tower and two dragons that are fighting each other; one dragon is red, the other is white. The figure continues to talk. "As soon as the Water from the Lakes pushes its way, the Dragons will start to fight. In their fight and their victory is hidden a great secret. The White Dragon will kill the Red one, and this is of great value for those who know how to recognize this in their lives. These are all Omens of what is on the point of happening."

*****

The way back goes easy; there is not much traffic on the road. On the long motorway through France, Jason can accelerate. The car flies over the road and he feels one with his sports wagon. The way is long and soon his thoughts return to his normal life and to what needs to be decided there. In fact, he needs to negotiate with Harry about the congress, because he just wants more free space. *Harry is a yellowbelly; he wants to head into another direction with the project. I need to firmly negotiate about this. I can send him a text message to see if he is available tomorrow.* The road is quiet and with one hand at the wheel and in the other one his mobile, his attention switches between the road and his text message.

Message back from Harry, who texts him about a commissioner who wants an article that proves that there are no dangers in using microwaves.

"But that contradicts our vision on the topic," Jason messages back. Harry answers that it brings in good money. "That is why we will write it."

Jason starts to tense up and gnash. *Where the hell does Harry want to go now?* Meanwhile, he passes the border in to the Netherlands. *Nice, just one more hour of driving and I will be back home again.*

Harry offers our expertise for a discount. We agreed on giving extra space to alternative therapies and treatments, making people aware of their choices. Harry walks at the hand of 'Big Pharma,' that branch of the medical industry that does not want to heal people, but make them dependent and captures them in a chemical corset, to be able to control them better. Then he realizes that this is a new insight to him. Since when did he become conscious of the politics inside of the medical industry? Somewhere deep inside he knew this, but it did not bother him enough. Why does he care now?

Embittered, he swallows his emotions and tries to send back a message, meanwhile keeping an eye on the road. It is dark on the unlit motorway. Then the clouds move away and the landscape becomes illuminated by the full moon. In the distance he sees the taillights of a car.

Again he types a few letters in to Harry. He glances at the road. To his amazement the clouds around the moon are blown apart and take the shape of two fighting dragons. It triggers something in Jason, and in a flash he sees a Red and a White Dragon, fully involved in a fight.

Then his attention is forcefully drawn to the road. When he tries to pass the car in front of him thoughtlessly, it gets a blow-out. Jason acts on his reflexes and steps on the pedal. The car next to him starts to sway and comes right at Jason. He feels a hard push at his right side and his tires lose their grip on the road. He slides from left to right, hits the crass barrier and bounces back to the road. The other car hits the crash barrier and tumbles over it. Time appears to come to a standstill. Every thought hovers crystal clear into thin air, thus enabling him to define exactly what he should do next. Swaying from left to right, he succeeds in getting control over the wheel. His car comes to a stop on the road shoulder. He scans his body, checks every muscle. Luckily he appears to be in one piece! He walks towards the place where the other car crashed to check it out. He starts to run when he sees thick black smoke coming from below the car hood. His heart starts to pound heavily, and again he acts on his instincts. He runs towards the car and tries to open the door. But it is locked tight. Jason looks through the windows and sees that the inside is filled with smoke. He looks around him for a rock to crash the window. A shrill screech sends the shivers through his spine.

*****

Restless I move in my sleep. I cannot fall into deep sleep. Something is nagging at the edges of my consciousness. Restless dreams move like clouds through my mind. Then I see the lightning flash hitting the tower and my attention switches to a scene on the motorway. In the deep dark clouds above the road two fighting dragons appear, a Red one and a White one. A car drives in full speed over the road and crashes another one. Then I see Jason's' face clearly appearing before my eyes. My heart opens and immediately I change into a channel. An enormous amount of energy streams through me, energy coming from the endless reservoirs of the cosmos. Through my heart I channel it and envelop him in a protecting aura of light and energy. It is pure force, love, and wisdom. I also feel the presence of the others.
"Dragon master, Lady of the Planetary Spirit, Walker-between-the-Worlds, quick! We need the Forces of Fire; Jason is amidst of his Test of Courage."
I have a trained team that is able to act 'At Will,' and who can instantly switch to the Temple in the Otherworld; the Old Family is always connected. That is why we are all warned when one of us needs the Powers. The switch is there immediately, and the four of us are on the spot giving everything that is needed at that

moment. I hear the Lady of the Planetary Deva starting with the recitation of the spells for the Alchemical Fire Transformations:

I ignite your Fires of Power to serve the Light;
To feed the Winged Human being
That lives within the depths of your soul.
Learn the secret of Resurrection,
Of human compassion and power when you are there to help.
Trust in the spirits and powers that work through you.
Show courage when you save the suffering human,
Kneel and surrender to my guidance!

*****

Jason pulls with full force at the car door and suddenly it opens. The smoke comes toward him and hits him full in the face. He uses the sleeve of his jacket to cover his mouth and nose, while he uses his other hand to pull the female driver from the car. Meanwhile the flames come out of the hood and it is extremely hot. Jason wants to support the woman and take her to his own car, but she refuses to walk and screams, "My baby! My baby!" Jason now feels the adrenaline rushing through his body. His heart is pounding like never before. Cold sweat breaks loose, every muscle is tensed, and his hair is standing upright.

*****

The spell of Earth is immediately followed by the one of the Dragon master, who activates the Power of Fire in Jason and supports him:

I ignite your Flame of Power to serve the Light,
To feed the Winged Human Being that lives in the depths of your soul. I
assist you and instruct you,
Change you into a Warrior of the Light.
I teach you how to protect the vulnerable and the sacred,
I turn you into a power for a Higher Mission;
Kneel and surrender to my guidance!

Jason no longer thinks; he suppresses his fear and jumps to the passenger part of the car. He pulls the door with full force and sees in a flash, amidst the smoke, a very small child hanging unconsciously in his seat. While Jason tries to loosen him from his infant carrier, the mother runs around panicking and screaming. She also jerks at the seat. The pitch black smoke fumigates from the car. The heat is unbearable! Jason sees nothing at all and there is very little oxygen. He takes a deep breath and gropes inside, pushing and pulling. Suddenly the chair comes loose and Jason tumbles backwards, along with the seat and the child. Around him there is only thick blackness, he cannot see anything. Coughing he crouches with the child, looking for a safe place at the side.

Meanwhile, all kinds of people come rushing to help, while bystanders call emergency services. Jason calls out to the spectators to see if there is anyone capable of reanimating. From the crowd a woman steps forward who loosens the child from his chair. She gently lays it on the grass and starts to give first aid.

Sitting in the grass, Jason watches the scene. His lungs are hurting, he has breathed a lot of smoke and he keeps coughing. His eyes tear while he is gasping for breath. In the distance he hears the sound of sirens. The sound comes nearer and blue flashing lights stop at a sort distance of the accident. People in yellow suits jump out of the ambulance. Jason hears fragments of the conversation about 'vital functions' and 'smoke poisoning,' while he is still coughing from the smoke. A first-aid worker puts a plastic mask on his face; *oxygen!*

"Please, come with us to the hospital," one of them says, and Jason is helped into the ambulance, together with the mother and the little boy.

*****

The Walker-between-the-Worlds follows the events with full attention and also his forces flow as waves of insight over the entire scene:

> *I ignite your Flame of Power to serve the Light,*
> *To empower the Winged Human Being*

That lives in the depths of your soul.
I teach you to work with the forces of resistance,
To transform challenges to Power and Wisdom,
I change you into a steady rock amidst of chaos,
I train you to apply the powers of your Warrior ship ethically.
Grow! In wisdom, power, and mercy,
Kneel and surrender to my guidance!

*****

How was this possible, how could this happen? In his mind, Jason relives all the details of the event. He was distracted during the drive. Would it have been possible to prevent this accident from happening? Time and again he plays the images before his inner eye and does not come to a conclusion. It started with the tire blowing out. *I accidentally happened to drive next to her when that happened. Would it have ended differently if my full attention had been on the road? Did I make things worse? Or was my presence lifesaving? I was not concentrating. In my mind I was arguing with Harry about the work. Am I guilty of this accident?*

*****

After the other three have empowered the magical working, I Melusine add my powers and I recite the last spell to activate the

Element of Air, the element of the Winged Human Being himself. I contact from the depths of my heart the most important quality of the Winged Human Being, the Spell of Love:

> *I ignite your Flame of Power to serve the Light,*
> *To empower the Winged Human Being*
> *That lives in the depths of your soul:*
> *I teach you the secrets of genuine love;*
>
> *Make love your greatest power, in every deed, in every work,*
> *In every relation with a living being,*
> *For every plant, animal, disembodied spirit,*
> *In every relation with a human being*
> *Kneel and surrender to my guidance!*

*****

Jason's heart breaks when his video of memories plays the accident before his inner eye time and again. He sees the boy sitting in the car, amidst of the pitch black smoke and the heat. Again and again he hears the crackling sound of the flames.

He watches the child that is still unconscious and connected to the oxygen. A nurse and a doctor work intensively to stabilize him. Shocked, he looks into the mother's eyes and thinks again. *Did I by my carelessness cause something irreversible to you?*

The ambulance drives through the city and Jason stares outside through the narrow window. He sees neon letters flashing by that are put high on the top of a building; 'Everything of value is vulnerable.'

*****

The last part of the spell still needs to be activated. But that can only be done in person. I need to do this together with Jason, with an explanation. I send him a text message that he needs to contact me quickly. Then I walk to my meditation room and ignite the four protecting candles on the altar.

*****

Meanwhile, Jason undergoes the full protocol of investigations once he arrives at the hospital. A police officer visits him to question about the accident and brings him the goods that he left behind on the crash scene. He opens the plastic bag and finds his car keys and his phone, which still works. He discovers the text message from Melusine.

I have seen the accident in my dream. I ask you to contact me urgently, as soon as you are capable. I need to speak to you! Melusine.

Jason raises his eyebrows. His eyes are wide open and his jaw drops. *How is this possible, this is impossible!* His hands start to shake and a nurse passes by. She pats him on the back. "You can go home, Mister Adams. I have good news. I have heard that the mother is completely healthy. The child, we will keep under our care for a few days. I have understood that without your courageous actions this accident would probably have taken two human lives. Fantastic that you were there to intervene. It happens so often that people become inert from fear and freeze on the scene. You are a courageous being, Mister Adams."

Jason realizes that the sun is almost rising. This will not become a working day. He is emotionally shocked. *Let me first go home and get some sleep.* He texts Harry that their appointment needs to be rescheduled, then arranges a cab and goes home.

There is no rest. Every time he tries to fall asleep, the images of the accident repeat before his inner eye. The brake squeal, the suffocating smoke, the screaming, and he is back amidst of the scene, like it is happening all over again. Jason feels guilty of the accident. *What if I would not have visited Tom? What if I would not have been distracted? What if I wouldn't have driven that fast? I need to change things in my life. That child could have died there in the fire, and I would have murdered my innocence! I would have caused an irreversible damage in my life and in the life of someone else. I would have had to live with those facts and with an unrepairable guilt!*

Jason tosses and turns, but doesn't find any rest. He needs to talk, talk, talk! With whom can he share this shocking experience?

Then he thinks about his work and the choices that he needs to make there; he is torn apart. *Do I dare to stand up for the people who need to undergo those medical treatments? Am I capable of being the spokesperson for that vulnerable group of patients, whose interests are in contradiction with the interest of the healthcare industry? Those patients are a symbolical child trapped in the fire; at risk of suffocating from the choking mist of a chemical harness, in the addictive grip of the drugs of the billionaires of this world. Do I dare to bring those poisonous protocols under the attention of the public? To become a warrior in the fight I need to be able to work from my heart, from a calling, from loving empathy. But I have that strangling guilt around my neck. What is the position of a modern employee? What is my position? Am I a disposable workforce?*

Jason thinks deeply about the conflict between his calling and ethics at one side, and the choking temporary contract and the conflict with his boss: what to do? Give in or move on? Listening to the call of his own lives mission? Or is there a third option? Can he open doors in the boardrooms, can he look those decision makers in the eyes and ask these ethical questions? Can his pen become his weapon in the coming battle? *Do I choose a peaceful life somewhere in the shadow, or do I follow my conscience and enter into the arena?*

Where do I find the power to withstand what will be coming towards me, when I choose this option? Jason asks himself desperately.

Then he remembers the text message of Melusine, with the request to contact her immediately, even urgently? He hardly knows her. He cannot bother her about the troubles of his accident, but it is really weird that she knows about it in the first place. Then he picks up his phone and dials her number.

*****

My telephone rings while I am writing. Normally I would let it switch automatically to the voicemail because it would break my concentration. Now that I see that it is Jason, I answer the call immediately. I chat with him and make sure that he stops by.

The coffee machine is running when the doorbell rings. I let him in straight away. He looks defeated. I invite him to sit with me on the couch and make sure that he feels welcome. When we both have a warm cup of coffee I ask him to tell me the entire story. First he tells me about the accident. I ask for all the details, because I am looking for the message of Myrddin. He beats around the bush until I say, "Jason, if I may I ask you, what kind of auguries preceded the accident? Because I received omens in my dreams, so you must have had them for sure. Did any strange things happen to you prior to the accident?"

Jason needs to dig deep into his memory. He tells me about his weekend trip with Tom. I let him give an account of the different activities he and Tom did together, and then he starts to tell the story of the chateau. My hair rises and immediately I have the feeling that here the keys are hidden. Questioning him, I dig deeper. I need to drill

Through a thick layer of resistance, because for one reason or the other, Jason has decided that the meeting with the guide and the lightning flash in the tower are not relevant. Finally, he tells the story with the lesson of the guide and shows me the photograph of the altar stone. I tell Jason, "That is the grave of Merlin that you have visited. I need to tell you about the 'Secret of Myrddin.'"

The Secret of Myrddin

"Myrddin, also called Merlin, was the Arch mage of Bretagne. He plays a crucial role in Western European Spirituality. Merlin is one of the great guides of the Inner Planes, he points out the way to the Otherworld, so seekers can travel safely through dangerous passages of their lives. He gives directions how to do that. You visited his altar stone and he reacted by appearing to you. That is very special! When he appears, like he did to you, he wants to pass on important spiritual knowledge. Knowledge that you will need during the next phase of your life. He told you the story of two dragons. That story is of the utmost importance.

The two dragons are part of you. Everyone has those two parts; they live in your soul. The Red Dragon symbolizes your survival instincts and the aim for personal power. The White Dragon represents your virtues, your talents, and your connection to goodness, to the 'Light.' The powers of the White Dragon aim at harmonizing you with your surroundings, with unity and an expansion of consciousness and awareness.
"When the Red and White Dragon start to fight, you are amidst of an inner conflict. Within you, a fight is going on between the outer world and the inner. The Red Dragon is your outer face. It represents your personality. It is the mask that you have created to survive in the world. It is your image, your false ego. This dragon connects you with a power that wants to corrupt you. The White

Dragon, however, represents the virtues that help you to achieve your goal in life."

Jason answers, "I have no clue what the mission of my life is about. I work to survive and try to have a pleasant life. That's it."

"I understand how you feel, because up until now your contact with the White Dragon is not properly developed yet. That is what Merlin warned you about. That is why he told you the story of the two Dragons under the Tower. The Tower is the construction that you made of yourself. Everyone constructs a personality that helps to survive in the world, but it has not enough contact with the soul. That is why you start to compensate. You compensate the unfulfilled needs of your soul with an outward facade. You are not the only one who does this. Look around you, there are millions of people who try to compensate their inner emptiness by keeping up appearances. Look at the fast cars, the beautiful women, the power suits. It is allowed," I say jokingly when I see his upset face. "But it does not solve anything. The inner emptiness is not being filled. You only get trapped in the consumer society. You do not feel fulfilled by it; you do not gain real self-confidence by it, because it remains an outer layer of glamour.

"Real fulfilment emanates from exploring and developing your individuality. That is a completely different development than the path of developing your personality and of false ego. Individuation comes from the inside. That part of you is in connection with the Transpersonal.

"The White and the Red Dragon are fighting each other. Once in the past the Red Dragon took over the entire inner space. Do you recognize that as a theme in your life? The parts of you that compete and compensate have taken over almost completely and chased away the forces of the White Dragon. For him there is no longer enough space left.

"This is a crucial fight, Jason! Do not hope that you can prevent your personality from dying during the fight between the Dragons. The White Dragon will burn the Tower of your artificial ego with its fire. Do not assume that your Tower, or whatever fortification you build, will be strong enough to prevent that. Your virtues, your qualities 'Sail at Sea;' this is an ancient expression to indicate that they are at work in your subconscious mind. At this moment they gather an enormous army that will bring justice. The White Dragon will defeat the Red one, and that fight will inevitably cause the death of your artificial personality. Jung called this the 'Death of the Hero.'[xi]

"Then the virtues – the parts of the personality who represent goodness – can come ashore. Merlin tells you that this battle is in full swing right now. The White Dragon will defeat the Red Dragon. His helpers will demolish your artificial personae and recapture the land that the Red Dragon seized long ago.[xii]

"What you went through last night was the Test of Courage. I was made aware of it through a dream. In my dream the Battle between the White Dragon and the Red Dragon led me straight to the scenes of your accident."

"I saw the scene with the Two Dragons in the clouds, right before the accident," Jason suddenly remembers.

"It takes an extreme amount of courage to get control over the Red Dragon, because it feeds on your deepest anxieties. You will be confronted with a lot of your questions and insecurities to integrate the cause of this accident into your life. Inevitably, you will need to look into the Mirror of your Self to find the answers. You will need to use a fine-toothed comb to go through your choices: starting from your private life until your choices and your vision on your work. What is your vision about your task in society? What myth do you live, Jason? What is your higher mission? Here, the search for the Stone of the Wise begins." And I point towards a polished rock that is lying on my altar. On the rock is written:

> It is a Stone and no Stone
> That entails the entire Art.
> Nature has created it,
> But didn't bring it to perfection.
>
> You will not find it on Earth,
> Because it cannot grow;
> It only grows in the Caves of Mountains.
> The entire Art is supported by it;
>
> Because he who owns the vapors of this thing,
> Owns the gold-plated splendor of the Red Lion,
> As well as the pure and clear quicksilver.
> He finds the Red Sulphur that contains it
> And thus holds the powers of the Fundament.[1]

"It is important that you learn how to Constellate instead of compensate. But first of all, I will give you a spell. Learn it by heart and repeat it a few times a day."

"What is Constellating?" Jason asks.

"I will give an evening lecture shortly, and then I will elaborate on that topic. It is too important, and the topic is too extensive to explain this in two sentences. You are with your head elsewhere anyway; first you need to process the accident. But this spell is important, because it will help you to gather the powers of the White Dragon. I have written it down for you," and I give him the note. "Read it in the morning, the afternoon, and in the evening." Together we read the spell:

I ignite the Flame of Power in me to serve the Light,
To empower the Winged Human Being
That lives within the depths of my being.
Search and find all treasures and bring them ashore in my soul.

Silver-plate the powers of Silver to reflect my inner-being,
Gold-plate the powers of Gold to illuminate my path.
Copper shed the power of Copper to enable me to see true beauty.
Speed up the powers of Quicksilver and teach me how to communicate,
Load me with the power of Lead to establish solid boundaries,
Teach me to strike when the Iron is still hot, so that I can defend myself.
Let me win the Bronze medal, for wielding pure power.

Purify the Metals; enable me to create with these valuables,
To make Priceless Jewels from Rough Stone, that I can wear.
I kneel and surrender to your guidance.

*****

6

THE WIZARDS WAR

London 2014

Jason is pacing up and down in his hotel room in central London. He stands still and puts his hands in his pockets. He looks over the glimmering grey roofs, wet from the characteristic London drizzle: an endless ongoing rain alternated by downpours. He turns around: the room is decorated with characteristic English rose wallpaper. The bed is done with a bedcover laced with ruffled edges, hanging down at all sides of the matrass. A straight bureau chair - definitely not meant to sit on for hours - stands in front of an electric kettle. Miserable bags with instant coffee stand 'inviting' next to a coffee mug.

He looks for a socket to charge his tablet. He doesn't find any other option than to pull the lits-jumeax aside, lie down flat on the floor and try to use the plug from the bed lamp to plug in his charger for the tablet.

He slowly rises and walks with the water kettle to the small bathroom. He looks at his mirror image; combs his hair with his fingers, then rubs over the stubble of his beard to feel whether he needs to shave before dinner. Looking at himself he ponders; *what is at the heart of my observations?*

He has just spent the second day on a congress about nutrition related diseases like diabetes, obesities, and anorexia. The specialists of today have made a deep impression on him. In his mind, he goes over the line of conferences that he has been visiting and thinks about the dilemmas. For months now he has been visiting various congresses in an attempt to find the cause of the big world crisis.

The problems are so amazingly big, so complex, and way too extensive to handle for just one man or woman alone. The area's in which the effects of the crisis occur are too different and the interests are too contradictory. On top of that, another difficulty surfaces; where the virtues start to fight the demon's party!

He sits down behind his tablet and starts writing an article for the magazine that sent him on this mission. He calls room service to deliver his meal, loosens his tie, and hangs his jacket on a hanger then starts to type.

It is late in the evening when Jason pushes the 'send' button to dispatch his article. Tired he plumps down on the bed. For a short while he zaps along some television stations and looks forward to tomorrow.

First check out, then he will visit the closure of the congress. After that there will be plenty of time to go to the British Museum. He has made an appointment to meet Wolf. By chance they can meet each other this afternoon in London, and possibly travel back

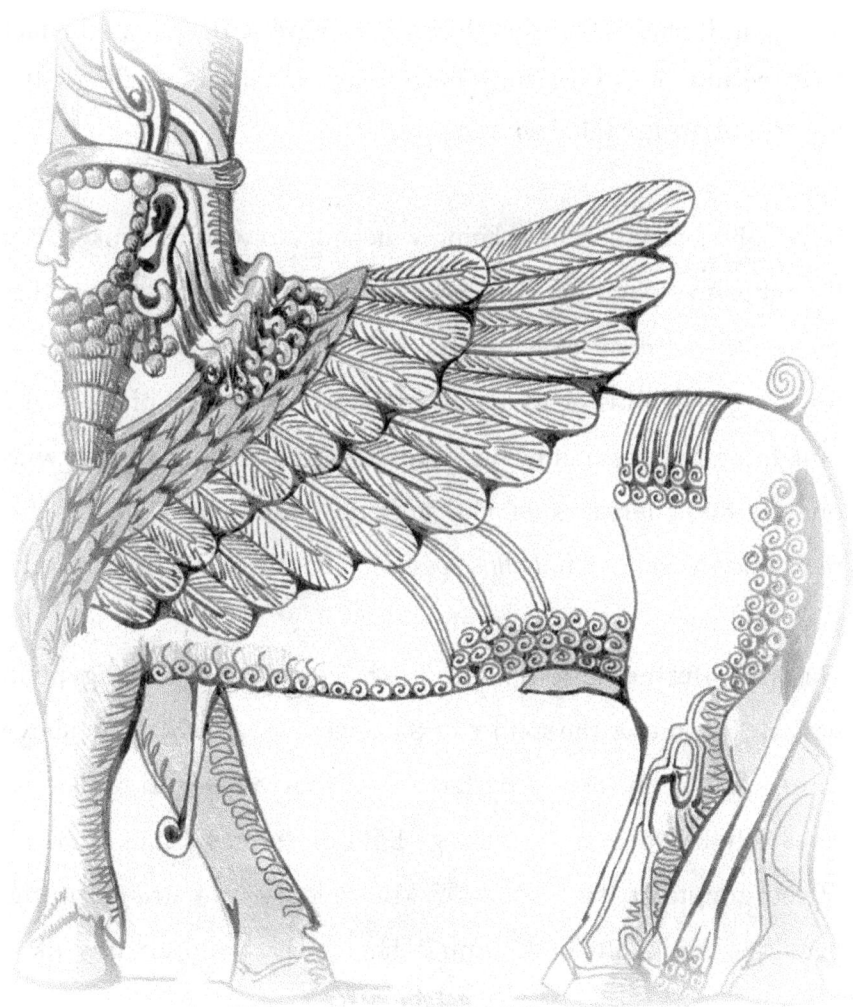

together. Wolf is a member of the group around Melusine, but Jason never got a chance to meet him earlier. Melusine is always full of commendation about Wolf. Eagle and Gabriella rave about him. He is very curious about what Wolf has to tell him. Then he sets his alarm, turns off the light, and falls in a dreamless sleep.

A thick fog in central London causes the air to look like dirty metal and the streetlights to be lit at 3.00 p.m. The British Museum looms up, and the hall looks like the entry of hell. Jason mounts the staircase and thinks that inside the museum it will be warm and light. It will distract him from the congress. In spite of the fact that the museum is warm, a haze hangs against the ceilings; the long corridors are filled with fog.

Suddenly, Jason feels he is being watched. No word is spoken, but thoughts go to and fro, and he realizes that the staring face that causes the stream of thoughts is bigger than human and is towering above his head. It is a human head on top of a winged bull. Jason realizes that he has established a telepathic contact with one of the guardians of the ancient temple of Ninevé. This realization shocks him. *Is this possible?* The statue appears to come alive and wants to communicate…

He walks further through the misty corridors to the Egyptian gallery. He studies the statues of the ancient gods who loom above him standing on their pedestals. Also, they appear to radiate an unearthly life-force in the strange light of the misty hall. A statue of red granite of the Goddess Sekhmet looks him straight in the eyes and suddenly in his mind he clearly hears an unspoken question. *Jason, whose side are you on, the side of the living or the side of the dead?*

Jason looks around. There is still no human being to be seen. Some fifty meters further a group of people are being led by a guide around the section antiquity. But they are too far away to catch anything of their conversation.

He is wondering; *what does this question mean?* Again he feels the alien mind-touch of the spirit of the statue. It is a weird sensation. The telepathic connection does not feel human, more catlike, but many times larger. He observes the statue from top to toe. It is a gigantic lioness, sitting on a huge throne. In her hands she holds an ankh. At the moment he studies her with full attention, the statue starts to radiate life. He searches for the point from where the thoughts appear to come and looks into the eye sockets that are inlayed with rock crystals; they appear to radiate a clear light.

Yes, I am real, Sekhmet purrs in his mind, with the energy of a seductive woman, like a lioness coming to nuzzle up. *Are you surprised that you can hear me? Folks think that I am dead, but I am alive, Jason!* The telepathic connection now feels as if he is hit by a small bump with a head, like a beloved animal comes begging for attention.

I ask you again, Jason, are you at the side of the living, or of the dead?

Jason shrugs his shoulders in a non-understanding gesture. *I don't know what you mean by that question*, he answers in his mind.

This question belongs to the fundamental paradoxes, Jason. There are seven basic dilemmas that a seeker on his journey to initiation needs to answer. When you become more sensitive to the energies from the unseen worlds, you will become aware of the fact that not only people and animals have consciousness. Matter is crystallized consciousness! Only the degree of awareness differs. You need an increased sensitivity to catch the frequencies of the deeper layers. The priests and the initiates from antiquity knew this. They worked with this principle and left their knowledge about it behind. In the world of the dead people assume that the universe consists of pure matter and that its nature is mechanical. They explain every phenomenon rationally. In the world of the living they assume that everything is fundamentally built from consciousness, and that matter is a more or less complicated receiving station for the endless consciousness of the interconnected whole. A human being is awake, an animal dreams, a plant sleeps, and a stone is comatose. On top of that, 'death' does not exist. The manifested world is just the top of the iceberg of a much larger spiritual reality.

The guided tour now comes closer and Jason experiences their presence as a disturbance. He hears the voice of the guide who tells about the superstitions of the ancient cultures that caused them to worship statues like they were gods.

Jason hears the roaring laughter of Sekhmet echoing through his head. In his mind she thunders, while an invisible claw taps him on the shoulder: *That is the mentality that I am speaking of.*
Jason grabs his head with both hands. *Am I freaking out? They call it hallucinations when you hear voices coming from outside yourself! Now I am walking through the British and I am communicating with a statue from Antiquity!*

He observes the corner of the statue, where the shapes of Sekhmet change over into the throne whereon she sits. On the throne he sees a fresh dandelion and a few dried daisies.

There are people who visit me more often and bring me flowers, Sekhmet says, now the internal voice is filled with pride, like a woman who receives flowers from her beloved.

The guided tour now comes straight at the statue and Jason turns around. He walks back to the hall with the Akkadian art and searches for silence in the presence of the Winged Bull. He looks at the stone statue, that quietly overlooks the abandoned corridor of the museum, and silently he releases an outcry for help in his mind towards the statue gallery and to his new friend, the Winged Bull of Babylon: *I am at your side*, he exclaims in his imagination. *Come to me, oh Winged Guardian of the House of Gods, open the doors for me!*[xiii]

Then the hollow sound of echoing footsteps resonates through the corridors, footsteps that come nearer. Wolf, a vigorous man in his fifties, dressed in a black overcoat with a shawl, dark short hair, deep blue glittering eyes, and grey temples, walks towards him with an inviting smile and outstretched hands.

"Hi, Jason, I knew I would find you here at this classical meeting place for magicians in London."

Jason rubs his eyes in disbelief and his eyebrows rise.

"The statues of the gods of the British Museum are famous within the magical world, they are alive and they call everyone who has become sensitive enough to catch their thoughts. Experienced magicians have learned to know this place as the most exquisite place to meet each other. This is a historical place, Jason. You will probably have established a contact with the Winged Bull. There are more living statues here."

"Are these phenomena from the Mirror Realm?" Jason asks.

"Where did you pick up that term?" Wolf remarks. "And what do you mean by it?"

"I read about the Mirror Realm in a book about Rosecrucianism. They strongly warned about the Thoughtforms and images that pollute the atmosphere around the earth. They would consist of paradises and hells that were constructed and dreamed about in former civilizations."

"We don't work with this concept. There are certain orders that use this word. They hold other opinions about the phenomena of the Otherworld. Our tradition has its own viewpoint about these phenomena and we handle them differently. Traditions hold different views and that is okay. It is important to know that the concepts of one tradition are not necessarily relevant in another spiritual system. We call this 'Mirror Realm' the Astral World, the world of the Wisdom of the Stars. We work with this realm intensively. We don't consider it to be polluted, but we work with it as a spiritual legacy, a source of wisdom, a gift from our ancestors. The Astral World is full of spiritual concepts. You need to know how to unlock this realm to retrieve the information, because without the key that unlocks the meaning of these images, you cannot benefit from that extensive spiritual richness of this realm."

These images loom up from what Jung called the 'collective unconsciousness.' They cause an expansion of consciousness, a connection with a different type of reality, wherein everything that exists, is interconnected by One Mind. The phenomena can be dangerous when you don't structure the flow of images, and without road signs you can end up in a mental confusion and chaos. But the road of initiation teaches you the language and the methods to work with this realm in a safe way, and to grow from it. In the past it has always been a source of inspiration and wisdom. Artists have painted this world; musicians have sung about it, the greatest investigations of humanity come forth from this realm. It is a source of growth, healing, and spiritual wealth wherefrom the most beautiful mythological stories developed. They still communicate the deepest wisdom to humanity through that 'Deep Spirit of the Cosmos,' from which we are all a part and that interconnects everything that exists."

By means of what we call 'Transpersonal Development,' you learn to communicate between your conscious mind and the Deep, between your ratio and the sub and super-consciousness. According to our experiences it is of the utmost importance to work with a roadmap in this world. When you use that map, you can safely work with these images."

Wolf points towards the Winged Bull and ads: "In Antiquity they constructed this type of statue very consciously. Nowadays we call them 'talismanic statues,' the word comes from talisman. The priest-magicians of the past researched the different energies of consciousness that are fundamental for spiritual development of human beings. They designed an idealized form to express these different energies, projected them onto the starry heavens, and called them constellations. This entire process was done by an extensive magical ceremony called 'Ascension.'

"Meanwhile, they made this type of sculptures for the in temples. The Winged Bull, for example, is a gateway to the energies stored in constellation Taurus. Through a complex ritual, which they called the 'Opening of the Mouth Ceremony,' the energies from the stars and the statues in the temple were linked. In this way the Gods were able to speak with humans. How powerful this method was, you have been experiencing when the Winged Bull and Sekhmet tested you," Wolf says smiling.

The two men walk through the museum and Wolf points out the differences between living talismanic statues and the imitations that lack the energy. They walk past the displays, filled with ancient Egyptian wicks, copper mirrors, clothing and jewelry, to a special hall that Wolf wants to show to Jason.
"This hall is important", Wolf says. "Here are the Ushabti's."
"What are they?" Jason asks.
"They are magical helpers. Statues were charged in the past with a task to do certain magical work on the inner planes. The process can be compared by learning how to drive a car. First of all, you need to consciously learn all the operations. By practicing all proceedings step by step, all the actions become automatic. In this way you learn to drive a car while at the same time having a conversation, or listen to the radio.
"By making an Ushabti for a quality, or to develop an ability to work for you, you no longer need to use willpower. By the making process, the assignment is programmed in your subconscious mind and your goal is connected to your 'automatic pilot.'"
"That sounds like an intriguing and efficient method. Are these Ushabti's still active?" Jason asks.

"Yes, absolutely. The British Museum some years ago offered the opportunity to sleep in this hall, because it is haunted. I am not sure whether that is still possible," Wolf answers, smiling.

"You can make powerful Ushabti's yourself. You take a piece of modeling clay. You mold magical images into the clay; images that you want to bring to live into life, to help you to perform a certain task. Everything that is done by the subconscious mind does not take energy from your conscious mind. By working with the unconscious mind, blockages can be detected and neutralized. It is a very powerful and efficient magical technique. Very convenient when you want to change jobs for example."

"How so?" Jason asks.

"In the past, when I myself started experimenting with these techniques, I made one myself. I did not think it through thoroughly enough. Within one week after the making of the Ushabti I was working at a different job. It went so fast! From that time on I was determined that I would build in barriers in the future, so that the Ushabti's would not start to do their work too early, without me having clearly finished the images of my wanted end result."

Wolf looks at his phone and says: "Jason, we need to leave for London St. Pancreas, we want to be on time for the train to the Netherlands."

Both men exit the museum and head for the Underground, to the train that will bring them to the international train station in the heart of London. The journey goes fast. They pass customer services and search for their places on the train. When it starts moving, the men lean backwards. The cadence of the moving train speeds up and the images at the outside environment flash along the windows in an ever quicker tempo.

"What did you do in London?" Wolf asks Jason.

"I am on a quest for the disposable truth," Jason answers with a serious facial expression.

"How so?" Wolf asks, interested.

The Disposable Truth

Jason starts to tell his story about the divorce from Joan, caused by his choice for childlessness. He talks about the confusion, when the images from the Otherworld increasingly threatened to submerge him. He pictures how he almost lost his inner balance because of an overflow of images from his inner world. How he needed to find a path between wisdom and folly.

He tells Wolf about the fundamental choice that he had to make; the dilemma between being dominated by the choices of his boss, or taking his life in his own hands. "I needed to choose to either accept the facts, or fight. I have chosen to use my pen as a weapon. This choice brings me to these strange crossroads where Sekhmet asks me whether I serve the living or the dead."

"That sounds intriguing," Wolf answers. "How do you want to answer her question?"

"I have no idea," Jason answers. "I have attended so many congresses lately, to try to discover the fundamental wound in our contemporary society, but I cannot find the final cause. Take for instance the world of security; here they need to deal with the issue of espionage on behalf of security. This will inevitably mean that our freedom will be limited drastically. What price do we want to pay to protect our freedom, when we destroy her in the process of safeguarding her?"

Wolf listens silently and attentively. He feels Jason's tension. Jason breaths deep and continues:

"Then the world of the criminality: until a few years ago, generally speaking, criminals belonged to the underworld. Nowadays, more and more, they start to acquire their places within the upper world, and take their seats in boardrooms. They play their games in the rat race for world power!"

Wolf can feel the passion of Jason. And Jason notices that he has an audience for this topic that is only understood by a few.

"I have investigated more areas of society. Searching for the stories of individual people. The energy world for example: One important part of the energy industry is on a mission for their religious 'truth' and wants to impose it to the rest of the world. Another part of this industry wrestles with the dilemma that a choice for sustainable energy implies, to make themselves obviate. A third party attempts to win the monopoly on energy. Their methods entail taking enormous risks of destroying ecological cycles definitely."

Jason now really gets angry, and with squeezed fists and tensed jaws he continues. "Then the world of the industry; they are caught in the race to be the cheapest. They create poisoned production processes, destruct animal life and cause illnesses on people."

Jason looks outside. His thoughts wander over the landscape, he points at the sloping hills that pass by at full speed; "The world food production industry gets into the hands of monopolists. They claim exclusive right on the production of seeds, water, vegetables, and meat." He looks Wolf directly in the eyes.

"Do you know that a part of the healthcare industry has an increasing interest in keeping people ill instead of curing them? Do you remember some years ago when an 'incredibly dangerous' flu epidemic was announced? The reports were so convincing that governments bought vaccinations for billions. But it turned out to be a hoax, a deliberate fraud!"

"While basic healthcare gets too pricy, new diseases are caused by the nutrition industry through additives; pesticides, genetic manipulation, and by adding addictive toxic substances to food. But the healthcare industry does not even investigate this area.

"On top of all this there is the financial sector, the power of the money that causes a split between the value of work and materials."

Jason sighs: "These are huge problems. They are too big. But the real question isn't even asked and that is; what is the real cause of the world crisis? What is the underlying cause that generates all the other phenomena?"

Wolf nods in understanding. "That is a very old question, Jason. That is the question that has been asked throughout history."

"This weekend I visited a congress about nurturing diseases," Jason says. "It was very informative. First of all; you are what you eat, and your health starts with the fact of whether you cook your food by yourself. Who cooks, determines the production process! That has consequences for all the steps in the production chain, right from the growing of the food reaching until the effects on your health. The closer the growing of food is to the consumer, the healthier it is. The more prefabricated, the more supplements are added by the food industry that are important to them, and the more toxic the end result will be."

"Examples of this are the conservation additives or the addictive substances that boost the sales. By means of advertising, the public is deceived by telling them that prefabricated food means progress. By singing lullabies in advert campaigns, the industry sends a message that everything is fine. The recipe is: first generate fear, and then offer a solution. The virtue – cheap food for everyone – is changed into a power game. Guess who is paying the price? You pay, with your health!"

Wolf looks thoughtfully; "For most people the most self-evident thing to do is to search for the cause of all trouble outside of themselves. That happens even in the most simple situation of having a fight with your own wife," Jason looks at him, surprised. That was completely not a reply that he expected.

Wolf continues, "Patterns that take place in families, mirror themselves within larger social environments; in organizations, countries, multinationals. That is the start of the Wizards War!"

Jason looks at Wolf, he is totally flabbergasted; "What do you mean?"

The fundamental illness that causes the world crisis is called 'humanity.'"

"That is too easy!" Jason exclaims.

"No," Wolf answers, "that is not easy at all. That is extremely difficult. Look at the cause of all conflicts, in your own life, in groups around you, it happens time and again: people do not solve their fundamental pains, but project the problem on another, or on circumstances. It is much easier to blame society or another group of people, then to search for the wound in yourself and take the full responsibility to cure it. That needs courage, Jason. Courage to search deep inside. It is the same amount of courage that you need, to enter into a fire and rescue the precious life that is at risk to be suffocated. You need courage to face the heat and the danger, to face up to the flames. The outcome is not sure, it is uncertain whether you will win the fight or lose, or even stay alive!"

"What do you mean by a Wizards War?" Jason asks.

Wolf leans forward and emphasizes, "Remember what I told you in the British Museum, when I explained to you how Ushabti magic works? I told you that it is extremely powerful magic, this type of magic is being used in this time and age as well."

"I don't see the connection?" Jason answers curiously.

"You take a product, it does not matter which one. It can be a political idea, or a product that you buy from a shop. You clothe it in packaging material, in beautiful colors. Then you surround it with magnificent ideas. You define what will go wrong in case you do not accept the ideas, or use the product; think of something disastrous! The next step is to charge your product with a song, a rhyme, and you repeat it endlessly in the media. You have created your perfect Ushabti, a magical helper that will do all the work for you. The associated ideas will sing in the minds of the receivers like hypnotic mantras. They will penetrate the subconscious mind of the public. The Ushabti does all the work and will inevitably penetrate into the collective unconscious mind, in the 'Otherworld'! Start to observe this, Jason. Welcome in the magical world of Thought Power, wherein the Power of the Word and Creative Imagination triumph. Observe how this works on all levels, starting from ordinary village gossip up to state propaganda, advertising, and political ideas. The principles are the same everywhere; generate fear for the opposition and reframe his behavior. The terrorist of one group is a freedom fighter to the others. Then create a positive frame around your own ideas and spread as many objects as you can with your desired associations. Modern advertising and propaganda are based on the same principles as ancient old talisman magic." Wolf leans back in his chair.

Jason absorbs the new ideas and thinks them through while he watches his mirror image in the window of the train. It is quiet for some time. Deep inside he knows that he as a journalist is also being used in this ruthless propaganda machinery... then he asks, "But how does this lead to the root of the problem?"

Wolf carefully chooses his words. He rubs his chin and frowns his forehead. With a deep voice, coming from his belly he says: "That involves a change in attitude, Jason. Train yourself, take back your autonomy. That will make you extremely powerful, because then you hold the key to personal happiness in your own hand. That will make you independent of the whimsical decisions of others. In your analyses of the world crisis, you have forgotten one important aspect: and that is the pollution of our psychological environment. Think for instance of the violence in the media or the intrusive sexualization. Your personal question becomes: How to nurture yourself psychically? How to protect yourself from unwanted influences? Do you watch violent movies, or do you listen to classical music? Do you feed yourself with intellectual wealth, do you have meaningful discussions? Or do you waste your time hanging on the couch, watching dumbed-down television shows? Do you spend your time with friends; do you grant yourself beautiful stories with a deep inner meaning? Praxis psychic hygiene, Jason! Invest in good things; good friends, healthy relationships, invest in your health, choose carefully what you eat. Be critical, choose what thoughts you accept, what cultural inheritance you soak in; work with transforming stories! Train your Thought Powers, Jason, and you will change your life. Teach it to others, and you generate a change of consciousness in society."

Jason reacts with disbelief; he tries to sort the thoughts that speedily tumble through his head. "Science did not prove the effect of the media on the escalation of violence and of sex."

Wolf smiles, "Wake up, Jason! Why do you think that billions of money circulates in the advertising industry, because it doesn't work? Count on it, that when people spend these amounts of money, they have assured themselves that it will be well-spent."

Jason rubs his face in an attempt to structure his thoughts and he looks Wolf in the eyes. "What is your opinion about this topic?"

"Every thought, every feeling is a genuine event to your inner-self. To your subconscious mind, it does not matter whether something happened objectively or not. Emotions cause real hormones to rush through your body and in this way even movies based on pure fantasy will influence you on your most basic, physical, and subconscious levels."

Realize that it is also possible to train your inner world. Start working consciously with Thoughtforms that influence your feelings, your thoughts, and your health. Working with these Thoughtforms is the basis for Hermetic Meditations, Jason. When you apply these principles in the right way, you build on a solid physical and emotional health and a protection of your boundaries. Meanwhile, you create a 'Stairway to Heaven,' winding around a stable Tower of your personality that will no longer crash by the opposing fighting forces of the Two Dragons, because they will now cooperate. Instead of working in a reality, wherein every few months a part of your life collapses and runs down to a level of spiritual, emotional, and physical poverty, you now build on a healthy fundament and fill your live with wealth."

Jason falls silent. This conversation offers a lot of food for thought. He looks through the window, to the ever-changing landscape. *When you pass through life like an express train, you suddenly become aware of the railway heading for an end station.* Jason sighs. Then he straightens his back and looks at Wolf. *This is an exceptional person. What kind of life would he live and what is his place in the group?* Jason decides to start asking questions.

"We keep talking about me," Jason says. "Now, how was your weekend in London?"

"Very inspiring," Wolf answers enthusiastically. "I have been to training for the advanced international core of the group. I have learned a lot. Melusine was in form. You simply don't get from where she acquires all her knowledge. She is an endless source of wisdom and knowledge."

"Why doesn't she travel back with us?"

"She went further to Glastonbury, because she will head another training in the center next to the Chalice Well. Within a few days she will fly back."

Then Jason bends forward and puts his hand on Wolfs' arm: "Wolf, I am participating for a while now with this group, I have a question that starts to become pressing: Who or what is Melusine?"

Wolf looks at him penetrating: "That question is not mine to answer. You need to ask her. But I can show you something that is the complete answer to your question, and meanwhile maintains your curiosity." Wolf grabs in the pocket of his jacket and takes out a completely worn out deck of tarot cards.

"Let me search," he says as he rumbles in the 'Book-of-the-Caves'[13] tarot deck. He shoves a card over the table towards Jason. Jason looks at the card 'Eternity.' Wolf says, "I will leave you with this riddle." And roaring with laughter he pats Jason on the knees, while he looks into his baffled eyes.

"Look at the time; it flies during an inspiring conversation. We have arrived in Dordrecht. I have parked my car here." Wolf starts to put on his coat and folds his shawl carefully in his lapels.

The train slows down and comes to a standstill at the rail station. The men say goodbye. Wolf waves a last time to Jason, who remains seated for the last part of his way back.

Jason is tired when he returns home. He leaves his suitcase in the hall. Unpacking can wait until tomorrow. His homecoming is immediately welcomed by Tiger, who runs with great speed down the stairs, and welcomes him, purring and nuzzling into his chest. Jason quickly answers some phone calls to finish his job and to inform that he is back home again.

*****

---

[13] I am currently working on the development of the tarot deck 'The Book of the Caves', you find the picture of Eternity at the end of this book.

At the side table lays the box with the ring. The Eye looks at Jason. The ring appears to be more life-like than usual. Suddenly he feels the mental pulling that he also experienced in the British Museum, when the Sekhmet statue started to communicate with him. Would the ring want to tell him something too? Jason decides to try it out; he puts the ring at his right pointing finger and relaxes. He walks through the steps of an exercise that Melusine taught him and let's himself glide away in a relaxation between the cushions of the couch.

An entity approaches him. He wears a grey beard and a white robe that reaches to his ankles. Jason clearly feels the mental click with the entity. The figure tells him that he is not from this time and age. He used to live in a physical body during the Middle Ages. He tells Jason that he holds important information for him, that he wants to share, now that Jason is capable of receiving it. He emphasizes that the technique he will teach him is extremely ancient and needs to be translated to his own time and age. The entity introduces himself as Pelagius. During the time that he inhabited a physical body he was a hermit. Pelagius emphasizes that he has written down his knowledge in a book. This book still exists, so the information can be verified. Then he starts to disclose a recipe.

Pulver Pelagiieremitae[14]

Take as much material as you need from the candles that have been blessed at the festival of the Presentation of Jesus at the Temple; wax from the Paschal Candle, and incenses and herbs that have been grinded into a powder on the day of the Ascension of our Lord. Take also some grinded blessed earth. Mix this with sacred water and salt. Sieve the powdered substance until it is completely grinded. Then place the mixture of these powders, together with the wax, in warm and blessed water, until the ingredients are mixed and have become one mass. After you have done this, you recite the Holy Father, the Ave Maria, and the Creed of the Apostles. With this holy water you can purify your house, your stables, and your ground. It will crystallize in the form of miniature crosses.[xiv]

When this is not sufficient you can also take an exorcist bath. For this you need to obtain fresh water from a river. Hold all the ingredients in your hands: take a small container with you that is filled with blessed soil, ashes that were consecrated during the mass in a church after fasting, and wax that was used during the Ascension Feast, and weave this together while singing prayers. Be careful *not* to mix it with any ingredients of a superstition, of an idle or suspicious nature, because demons will get attracted by these very ingredients.[xv]

---

[14] Powder of the Hermit Pelagius

Then the vision disappears and leaves Jason with yet another riddle. He writes it down immediately to assure that he cannot forget anything. Then he thinks what to do with this information. *I'll email this straight away to Melusine. I am very curious what she has to say about this.* And with a few mouse clicks he sends off the information that he got through the ring.

*****

I see the email coming in. I notice that Jason is online. *Let's try to contact him straight away on Skype.* I push the button, I hear the typical bell sound of Skype and then I see Jason appearing on my screen.

"Hi, Melusine," says the voice at the other side.

"You got some really good information from the Otherworld," I answer.

"Do you think so?" Jason says. "I find it rather confusing. I do not understand it at all. But you do?"

"A clear case," I smile broad when I see the confusion at his face. "For me it indicates that you are ready for the next part of your training. I have had an enthusiastic report from Wolf, who told me that you communicated with the Spirit of Sekhmet and the Winged Bull in the British Museum. It is time for you to learn how to create a Sacred Space that is free from any outside pollution. Pelagius is very clear about this."

Jason notices that Melusine speaks about Pelagius as if he is a real person. When he vocalizes this thought, I answer immediately, "O yes, for sure. He was a very important source of inspiration for

Trithemius, when he was physically incarnated. Trithemius is one of the most important monks that practiced the Hermetic Tradition. He was the teacher of Agrippa von Nettesheim!"

Again names appear that are completely new to Jason.

"You have work to do, Jason. Hermeticism did not fall down from the sky. It has a long history. It arises from the mists of Antiquity. You find traces of this tradition in the oldest written documents that exist on earth, like the pyramid texts, and the most ancient astrological texts from Sumer. It was passed on from mouth to ear through every generation, and written texts have survived the ages. This enables us to trace our tradition down throughout the entire history. The West has its own Wisdom teachings, Jason, older than the Christian sources, independent of Judaic sources. The Hermetic Mystery Tradition goes back to the age of Thoth!

"But before I wander off…we need to make an appointment shortly with the core of the group, because it is time to teach you how to create an effective magical circle around you, to protect yourself effectively against influences of a 'superstitious, idle or suspicious nature.'" I smile. "Bring a lantern with a candle tomorrow evening with a semi-precious gemstone included in the wax. Do you have something like that? And don't forget to bring your ring."

We run through the details and then I end the conversation.

The Paradise Garden

The group meets in the temple building that Jason visited earlier. Now, apart from me, there are only four people present: Dindrane, Michael, Eagle, and Jason. They walk past the coffee room; there is no time to chat at the bar.

I push the button and notice Jason's surprise when the bookcase swings sideways and gives access to a passage and a hidden room.

Jason looks around. He sees a large hall with a floor of black and white tiles and a cubical altar stone in the middle. Around it stands a ring of pillars. At both sides of a high chair stand a white and a black pillar. Straight above the chair hangs a burning lamp, made of stained glass. It depicts the same eye as his ring! Suddenly he hears words with his inner ear; *For Your Eye Only*... of course, the One Eye is the Eye of God. The Spirit of the Deep looks directly at him at this place. Against the walls hang images that depict the constellations of the Zodiac.

"Put your ring on the altar, Jason. Come, sit next to me and watch what happens." I point out some important symbols of the temple space.[15]

"It is important that you learn how to keep your 'Sphere of Sensation' clean and to protect yourself from unwanted influences from outside. Learn how to intensify your connection with the 'Spirit of the Deep.'"

To his amazement Jason watches how the images from his visions start to take a solid shape. He listens in awe how Melusine, after the opening ceremony, proceeds with the ritual that he kept seeing in his imagination. He feels the energy coming in waves, washing through his body. It is benevolent, healing, hypnotizing. While he

---

[15] Read "The Temple of High Magic" by Ina Cüsters-van Bergen for the explanation about the temple space and the creation of the Magical Circle.

listens to the words, the images in his mind melt together with the outer events and become solid.

I stretch out my arms towards the illuminated eye above the high chair and turn around to look at all the images of the Zodiac. With a deep and resonating voice I incantate:

> *"Oh, House of Stars, dressed in lapis lazuli blue.*
> *Oh, holy city called Atlantis,*
> *Founded on an island in the Cosmic Ocean.*
> *Cathedral build for the rites of Magicians and Priests,*
> *House wherein the incantations for Heaven and Earth are recited.*
>
> *We call upon the Winged Human Being*
> *Appear in our midst, reflect our destination.*
>
> *Let us connect ourselves consciously*
> *With this being, the Highest Light within us.*
> *Let us perform the Sacred Magic*
> *That the One gave to the Sages of the Times.*
> *We dedicate a candle with a precious stone to the Great Work."*

All participants now put down their candles on the altar. I look at Jason. He too steps forward and puts down his candle on the cubical stone. Together with the other initiates we recite:

> *"A candle charged with powers to Serve the Light,*
> *To awaken the Winged Human Being*
> *Who lives in the depths of our souls.*
> *Being that knows about the patterns of the past and of the future,*
> *That resonates in harmony with the Most High,*
> *That vibrates on the rhythm of the most Holy Will.*
>
> *Being that has access to the past and to things long forgotten.*
> *Who know what will come and can interpret the omens!*
> *That knows how to divide false from true friends.*
> *I kneel and surrender to your guidance."*

Dindrane continues. She holds the place, where in Jason's earlier visions the Lady of the Planetary Deva appeared. Her voice sounds clear and self-assured:

> *"We create a Candle of Power to serve the Highest Light,*
> *To awaken the Winged Human Being*
> *That lives within the depths of our selves.*
> *Who illuminates and initiates our true nature*
> *And knows the essence of every spirit,*
> *every human being and every animal.*
> *Who advises us from its all-knowing wisdom.*
> *I kneel and surrender to your guidance."*

Michael now stands at the place of the Warrior-Monk, and also his voice echoes through the hall and fills the entire space:

> *"I donate a Candle of Power to serve the Highest Light*
> *To call upon the Winged Human Being*
> *That lives in the depths of our souls.*
> *That gives us access to sacred caves,*
>
> *To mines where hidden treasures lie buried,*
> *Into the deepest depths of our quest.*
>
> *Thou who leads us to those depths*
> *And who helps us to do the work that needs to be done,*
> *Who helps us getting access to these inaccessible areas,*
> *Who helps us with our work of transformation,*
> *I kneel and surrender to your guidance."*

Then Eagle stands, and with an energy that Jason never discovered behind his fragile looks, he now fills the entire space with his presence. He stands at the place where Jason saw the Walker-between-the-Worlds. Jason is filled with awe when he hears the texts. He gets goose bumps, because the energy increases every time another person speaks:

> *"I donate a Candle of Power to serve the Highest Light*
> *To awaken the Winged Human Being*
> *Who lives in the depths of our being.*

> *Being who knows the true nature of all our visions,*
> *Regardless whether they appear in glass or in crystal,*
> *In sacred wells, in the air, in rings,*
> *In wax, in fire, in the Moon, in the lines of the hand.*
>
> *I listen to your voice and follow your instructions.*
> *You who guides the spirits of the animals*
>
> *And puts them on my path as guides,*
> *Regardless whether they have the form of a lion,*
> *An eagle, a snake, a unicorn, or a dragon:*
> *I will act upon the wisdom they teach me.*
> *I kneel and surrender to your guidance."*

Now I give Jason a piece of paper; "Here, now it is your turn." Jason reads and experiences. He feels the energies rising through his spine. Suddenly all the attendances become overshadowed by an aura of power. He sees how I melt together with the High Priestess from his visions, and starts to radiate a supernatural light. Also, the others now look completely different. Jason blinks his eyes, is it true what he sees?

I give him an encouraging push, and then he steps forward and recites the text:

> *"I create a Candle of Power to serve the Highest Light.*
> *To awaken the Winged Human Being*
> *That lives within the depths of our souls.*

*Teach me the keys to the Twelve Hours of the Day
And the Twelve Hours of the Night.*

*Grant me the power to get visible and invisible.
Teach me the Sacred Magic of the Light.
Grant that my magical rituals cause effects:*

*To heal the bewitched and to calm down magical storms.
Being of Light that knows every book that was ever written,
Regardless whether it got lost or disappeared.*

*Who teaches us the Book of the Night and the Book of the Day,
The Book of Nature and the Book of Magic.
The Book of Alchemy and the Book of Healing,
The Book of Life and the Book of Death.*

*Who leads the spirits that supply us with food for our bodies:
Of food and drinks, bread, meat, wine, fish, and cheese,
That keep our bodies healthy,
So that we have time and space
To develop ourselves through the Great Work.
I kneel and surrender to your guidance."*

Jason now feels the energy physically; he feels crackling and sparkling. He sees colored fields of energy surrounding the attendees. In my function of High Priestess, I step towards Jason, and pick up his ring from the altar. I bless it while I call it by its name; Lapis Sancti Magi. Then I offer it back to him. Jason puts it back on his finger. Completely and expectedly he gains access to the Otherworld. There isn't any difference any longer between his reality and his visions. They now completely melt together, without any conflict. Love, power, and wisdom wash through him. Insights surface in his mind and he has no clue at all where they come from. He receives images and a flood of thoughts flows through his head with a content and a quality that he never experienced earlier in his life.

His perspective shifts and he experiences himself standing amidst of a Ring of Sacred Fire. His four comrades guard four gates; they look as if they are towering angels, huge, Keepers of the Gateways between the Worlds, as guardians giving access to a different level of reality. He feels he receives a deep connection to that deep layer of consciousness.

The Lady of the Planetary Deva stands amidst of a channel of energy, filled with fertility and health. The Warrior-Monk brings in a flood of passion, of rapture and inner mission. The Walker-between-the-Worlds changes into a portal towards intuition, creativity and deep feelings, flowing inwards on the resonance of an inner certainty and knowing.

As High Priestess I now step forward and purify his Sphere of Sensation[16] with incense and suddenly Jason perceives thoughts

---

[16] The Hermetic Mystery Tradition has a vocabulary of its own. The 'Sphere of Sensation' is similar to what in Eastern Mysticism is called the 'aura'.

with an unknown force, he feels exactly what Thoughtforms are pure, and which ones are polluted with mixed interests.

Jason feels how the powers of the Four Elements of the Wise flow through him and how he himself starts to pulsate and give off energy as well.

I watch him and nod my head encouraging to everyone. Then it is time to close down the ritual and leave the temple space. One by one the participants pick up their lanterns and walk out in a slow and rhythmical pace.

Michael returns the bookcase to its place. Jason looks around him. When one is not aware that there is a hidden space, you have no clue at all about the presence of the consecrated temple room deep in the heart of the building. At his forefinger he still wears the Lapis Sancti Magi. The stone is flickering and the eye looks at him. *What was it exactly, that happened just yet?* He asks himself.

"It is time to have a decent meal," Michael says. "It was a beautiful and powerful ritual, but now we need to take some time to get properly grounded again."

"That is a good idea," Dindrane answers. "I will go to the Chinese restaurant around the corner and get us some food."

While Eagle starts to carry dishes and set the table, Jason and I sit down to evaluate the past events.

"I cannot deny what I have experienced just yet," Jason confesses. "That was awesome and inspiring. But what exactly was it?"

I look at him very seriously and say: "You have contacted the Deep, Jason. People nowadays have fallen asleep to this reality. It is important to awaken them to this level of life again! That is the goal of our Great Magical Work. That is why we reawaken the Old Family! We want to wake up the world to the age-old pattern of equilibrium, truth, and harmony. We want people to regain access again to the All-knowing Field. Our job, Jason, is to help people to open themselves again and to become channels for this wisdom. Thus, they can make their choices with love, power, and wisdom, in harmony with the Planetary Deva. It is of the utmost importance that people learn to handle their energies safely, when they are woken up by the Kundalini force; they need to be guided through this process of Metanoia. Thus they can develop their antennae for the Heavens, whilst staying firmly rooted in the Earth.

"Deep inside of the souls of the people, there is a place where everything is exactly as it has always been. The Egyptians called this place Tep Zepi, Eternal Time. When you work on that level, you are in a direct connection with the most fundamental primordial pattern. Then Gods and Angels appear, and you can communicate in spirit. The priest-magicians from Antiquity have used this Eternal Time to store their most powerful talismanic images with the most primary meanings. On that level of consciousness they constructed gardens."

Jason raises his brows in a big question mark. "Ever heard of the Garden of Paradise, Jason? There is more behind this story than apparent on the first view.

"You have now collected all the ingredients for your first garden. It is a place in the subconscious mind, wherein you can sow, plant, and harvest. This magical place is connected to your ring. The circle of gold is symbolic for the path that the Sun travels throughout the year. The four letters of the Tetragrammaton are connected to the four elements: Earth, Fire, Water, and Air. When you have gained control over these elements in your life, you have created a magical field, your 'Sphere of Sensation'. By doing this, you have also generated a free space in the center. This is the place where the fifth element rules; there is the place of your heart. The Eye of the Deep looks right into your heart. The Eye is a symbol for the Spirit of the Deep."

Jason looks to the stone of the Lapis Sancti Magi and looks at the shining eye of the star sapphire.

The Spirit of the Deep

Then he asks: "But why all the fuss, to what end does this serve?"

"A fair question," I nod. "When you thoroughly build your magical circle, according to the rules of the Art, you are less likely infected by the Wizards War and all the spells that are conducted around on the psychic levels. From then on you can start to build your Contacts with the Spirit of the Deep, using the Talismanic Images. The Contacts will keep you connected to the Laws of Humanity and the Planetary Spirit. The Magical Circle is an utmost Sacred Space.

"The Magical Circle has a second important effect. By calibrating the events of the outside world to the happenings of your interior world, through Transpersonal Development, you increasingly will develop a stronger grip on the material effects that you cause. Transpersonal development uses special meditation techniques that will bring you into contact with the underlying interconnected layers of the Collective Subconscious Realm.

Through a process of synchronization between the Deep and your life, you slowly start to learn how to create. You get more insight in your mission in life, through visions. In this way, you will develop a vision that enables you to translate your ideals to your environment.

Can you imagine what that means, when you can exert your profession from that vision? When you work inspired by your Contact with the Spirit of the Deep?"

Jason tries to imagine what the effect could be on his work. *My boss will not accept a story like this when he enters the newsroom on Monday morning.* "They will think I am ready for the funny farm," he says loud and clear.

"Of course, you cannot talk about this in such a way to your boss," I roar with laughing.

"You need to translate your insights to your world, to your work, to the Spirit of our Time. By doing so, you will start to generate more value in your own field of expertise. The training on the Inner Planes is an instrument, to connect the Heavens (that is the Deep) to the Earth (your daily life). The Gardens from the Hermetic Mystery Tradition are mandala's to work with. Gardens, Castles, Towers, and Magical Circles; they all are Western Mandala's."

I think deep how to explain the effects to Jason. I put my finger against my forehead to concentrate my thoughts. Then I look at him and say:

"The images that play off deep inside, they are part of a program that runs in your soul. By emotional wounds or inner struggle your access to this program can get blocked. When you tune into the Talismanic Images of the Deep, everything starts to flow again. This even causes physical effects. Your hormonal system gets influenced by it, your feelings, you will choose otherwise, make different decisions. This will cause different events and outcomes. Your subconscious mind filters. From the millions of stimulants that reach you every second of the day, your subconscious mind chooses what information it lets pass through to your conscious mind. Even before you have the chance to make a conscious decision about it. The Deep determines the myth that you live in. That is your life's program. When you train your imagination you will get more effective and will generate more flow."

Then Dindrane walks in with a warm meal, and a cheerful clinging of crockery fills the room. Everyone takes a seat at the dinner table. Eagle upholds the dishes and says jokingly to Dindrane: "Lady of the Planetary Deva, can you fill these pentagrams with the fruits of the Earth?"
Michael takes the knives and says, "Let me distribute the swords. To what element would the forks belong?"
"Water," Eagle answers.
"Water? No that is the spoon," Dindrane exclaims.
"That too," Eagle says, "but the fork reminds me of Poseidon's Trident."
Everyone is laughing, the cracking bags are opened and they start with their delicious evening meal.

Jason remains quiet during the meal. He needs to process all the information. Then he looks at me and says, "I am still a bit confused. I don't know what it is what I experienced, but I cannot deny it. I need to place it. How is all this connected to the world of Jeanette and Ellie?"

Jason starts to tell his story about the situation at work, where the receptionists, Elly and Jeanette, were talking about unicorns and rainbows. "How does their world connect to ours?" he asks.

Eagle smiles. "Yes, I understand your confusion. There are more entrees to the Sacred Tradition. Some people get the contact through fantasy, movies, tarot cards, or magazines."

Dindrane says, animated: "The initiates of the past have helped to develop all kinds of products, so that people can access the Wisdom Tradition in a playful way. There is material for scientists, artists, priests, and for lay people, and thus also for Elly and Jeanette."

Michael agrees. He says enthusiastically: "The most important thing is that people develop a feeling for it in their own way, according to their personal taste."

"Absolutely," I agree. "Elly and Jeanette already started feeling the effects of the Sacred Tradition. In a playful way seekers can slowly begin the practice, until the point comes where some of them become really willing to jump in at the deep end. That happens when they take themselves and their experiences bloody seriously, and are willing to go for it. Then they become candidates for the temples."

"What kind of temples?" Jason asks interested.

"The Mystery Temples, they still exist," I answer ...

The Dansing Beauty

7

THE DANCING BEAUTY

Restlessly Jason tosses and turns in his sleep. Trails of dream images move through his mind like clouds. His dream leads him to after an interview for the magazine *Caduceus*, he walks out of an office building, arrives at a footpath and starts to walk. The walkway stretches out endlessly in the direction of the horizon. The flats from the city center make way for the houses at both sides of the road. He walks huge distances and passes the border of the city. The stone desert changes gradually into a dune forest. Curiously he continues and notices that his feet now move through loose sand. He hears a rustling noise and, completely unexpected, a large black animal walks towards him.

It is a wolf. *What is it doing here?* The animal approaches him and Jason looks in its yellowish eyes. The wolf sniffs and strolls around him, as if he wants something from Jason. In the far distance Jason hears the howling sound of even more wolves, it touches him deep inside. Trails of thoughts penetrate his dream, an invitation to join the journey. *Where does it go?* Jumbled images follow; they don't make any sense to him. He decides to follow the wolf, right through the hilly dune forest. The animal immediately leaves the pavement and rushes through a wilderness of plants and bushes. Jason follows it through the brush. When he leaves the normal scope, branches sway past his face. At some passages he really needs to bend low, or climb, to find a way through the tight forestation. Uphill, downhill, past loose sand, and across swampy plains. Finally he reaches the last hilltop and overlooks the coastline. He oversees the grandness of the landscape at the North Sea coast from that last dune. A river broadens and causes broad forelands, wherein strange types of reed and rare bryophytes cover the brackish bottom.

Suddenly, in what seems to be out of thin air, more wolves come running and surround him. It is as if the pack made an appointment to gather here at this hilltop. He feels in his mind how the animals contact him; an urgent request to follow them to the rough uncultivated areas of the coast. *What a strange place this is, where rivers merge into the tides of salt and brackish water, nature's laws become whimsical and unpredictable.*

At the far end, a lonely pier stretches out over the surface of the waters. Jason follows the wolves to the edge. Around him he hears the trotting sound of paws on ramshackle weathered wood. The waves change into wild foam while they beat against the breakwater under the pier. They splash upwards and merge with the sea mist.

At the horizon an old-fashioned wooden sailing boat appears. Huge white sails loom up from the mist and mark out the ship against the air. On the sail is pictured a symbol. Jason recognizes it when the ship has come near enough. It is a stylized red rose with green leaves and a golden core. The boat approaches the pier and moors. Jason stands in the water surrounded by the rough tidal waves, surrounded by wolves and wonders what this is all about.

Suddenly, the wolf that guided him to this place changes his shape into Wolf. He smiles at him. The dream-Wolf gesticulates to follow him aboard of the ship and walks in front of him.

Jason now becomes aware of the cracking sounds of the enormous wooden masts and of the clasping noise of the wind in the sails, the rushing and splashing waters, and the screaming seagulls above his head. At the front side of the deck Jason sees a wooden steering wheel, and behind it a cabin. On the door of the cabin is a picture of the same rose.

Jason looks through the artistically carved wooden windows and discovers a dais in the room, completely surrounded by roses. Wondering, he turns around to ask Wolf what all this means.

"This magical ship carries a secret. It contains a part of your soul that you have forgotten. Go inside and remember her; she is your sister."

Wolf turns around and disappears in to the thickening sea mist. Jason now is utterly alone on the ship.

Then he hears strange words echoing through his brain:

> *Become enchanted by that Beauty*
> *That reveals its serenity*
> *in sorrow and in darkness...*

He decides to enter the cabin and take a look. When he carefully opens the wooden door, the sound of rusty iron hinges reverberates. The hinges slice, and the sound of the cracking wood deadens in the thick fog. He approaches the dais and immediately shrinks back: it is a bed, wherein to his amazement, Dindrane lays asleep, naked, between the roses. Her red hair fanned out like a wreath around her head. His eyes wander over her beautiful body, his breath stops at perceiving her unearthly beauty. In her arms she holds a huge sword. On the handle is the picture of a pelican that has picked itself a bloody wound, from which she feeds her three young chicks.

Jason looks around in the cabin. The most striking is the ceiling; it is completely covered with shiny copper.

He walks around the dais and sees at the head of the bed an inscription is carved in the wood. Jason walks towards it. With his hand he wipes away the cobwebs, and tries to read the message.

> *Behold, on this bier Beauty is placed;*
> *The beautiful woman that deprives so many man*
> *Of their wealth, honor, blessings, and welfare.*[xvi]

Under her pillow Jason sees a letter. He shrinks back in fear, and freezes; he does not know where to look. He has the strong feeling that he sees something that is not meant for his eyes. His neck hair rises and with a shock he wakes up from his dream.

*****

Jason turns on the light and sits upright. He moves his hand through his hair, and rubs his face to wake himself up. He looks at his alarm, half past six. Time to wake up and write down this strange dream. *I don't know what it means, but it is of the utmost importance,* Jason decides.

The coffee machine rattles and when he closes his tablet, Jason starts to prepare himself for a new day. He has an appointment with his old friends Rudolph and Robin to go partying in Rotterdam. It has been a while since he saw those two blokes. He looks forward to a day of fun. Today is the day of the summer carnival. He intends to also go as a journalist, because this colorful festival always provides a nice article. They have made an appointment to meet at one of the terraces of the old harbor. Jason parks his car nearby and walks the last part towards his destination. While he walks passed the streets, he sees a girl finishing her make-up while looking in her car window. A robust mama, dressed in a colorful dancing outfit, wearing a feathered hood, helps her child tenderly, stepping into a similar outfit. Small groups of party animals walk by, dressed in similar cyclamen colored dresses. Their skirts flutter around their legs in the wind. Giggling girls clothed in feathered dresses pose proudly for the photographers.

The usually so businesslike city of Rotterdam, slowly changes into a miniature Rio de Janeiro. You can hear the sounds of drums in the distance, beating the rhythm of the samba. Jason walks through the crowds, along with the masses of merrymakers. Everyone is on their way to participate in the spectacle. He feels how the adrenaline slowly spreads through his blood and starts rushing through his veins. When passes the bridge he sees four waving hands. Yes, Robin and Rudolf appear in the crowds. The men greet, petting each other at the shoulders. They don't take the time to sit down somewhere. Now that the companionship is complete, they enter into the city, and start to move from place to place.

They witness a fire-eater, sparely dressed in a golden costume fascinating the crowds by blowing huge fire flames into the air. They visit several stages, where the public swings on the rhythm of the drums. They penetrate deeper into the partying crowds, until they arrive at the starting point of the Grande Parade.

Large floats full of dancing women dressed in tiny bikini's form a whirling mass of rhythmically moving fabrics, fake jewelry, and large feathers in all the colors of the rainbow. Moving breasts, barely covered with plastic flowers, and swinging bottoms accentuated by sexy strings, cause tiny little bells to tinkle.

Jason has a good time. He dances the samba with unknown beauties. Rudolph and Robin are glad to see this. They try to persuade Jason to take advantage of the opportunity to make some new contacts with the female part of the population.

Rudolph pokes him with a friendly gesture. "You have been alone for a while now, friend, isn't it time to look for someone to love?"

Robin wholeheartedly agrees and says: "A festival like this is an excellent opportunity to research your market value. Jason, it is time to try out your seduction skills."

Jason looks around him; *they definitely have a point! The breakup with Joan is a while ago now.* Then he sees her dancing, at the other end of the hall. Long dark hair and a beautiful short dress that shows off her gorgeous long legs. Along her neck she wears a silver chain with semi-gemstones in the colors of the rainbow. She looks him straight in the eyes and smiles sexy. He suppresses his tendencies to walk directly towards her, but he stays calm and moves unobtrusively in her direction. He pokes her 'by accident' in such a way that he softly caresses the sensible spot on her wrist.

"What is your name," Jason asks while he deliberately lowers his voice as a secret weapon in the flirtation.

She smiles lovely, "Salomé," she answers. "And yours?"

"Jason," he answers. Then the drums tempt her to continue the dance, and she looks at him invitingly. Jason follows her. Rudolph and Robin withdraw discretely and give him space to start a new chapter in his life...

*****

The next day Jason has an appointment with Melusine. He has asked her to tell him more about his ring, the Lapis Sancti Magi. Thus, she has invited him for this Sunday afternoon to a meeting with a small group. He walks over the cobbles, watches how the pleasure crafts cheerfully float on the waters, fastened to green cast-iron buoys at the waterside. Cozy flower flowerpots filled with geraniums adorn the windows of the houses. Even the bannisters along the bridges are decorated with flower pots. He approaches the now familiar house at the canal, and knocks with the mermaid doorknocker. The door is opened by Gabriella, who warmheartedly greets him. He looks around and sees trusted faces. Leo, whom he met earlier at the group meeting. Lucas, with whom he had a discussion. Slowly a small group gathers in the front room of Melusine's house.
Jason is fascinated by this place. The mediaeval house is a monument. The robust antique roof beams made of oak wood support the house in an artistic pattern, and elegantly contrast against the white plastered walls. His eyes move along the black and white tiled floor. He sees the indoor fountain, and stops just long enough to listen as it makes a burbling noise. The water comes from a trumpet shell that is held up by a mermaid made of foundry iron. The water-basin is formed like a seashell. The lotus flowers drifting on the water are now fully opened. He studies the

pictures with the mythological scenes that hang on the walls. A new painting is added to the collection: a mediaeval scene. It depicts a woman standing in a meadow. At her feet are white lilies. Lying in the grass is a second lady, wearing a gown with a rose pattern on it. Her eyes are closed. Above her head flies a dove, holding a thurrible in its beak. Noblemen have gathered around her and bend forward in a gesture of honor. Straight opposite of this picture is the bookcase with the hidden temple space behind.

Lucas shows him his seat. The chairs in the room make a full circle. One chair is obviously reserved for Melusine. Then the doorbell rings and Wolf enters in a hurry, excusing himself that he got delayed.

*****

Today's lesson is an important one. It is crucial for the five people I have invited. I dress in my long narrow sea-green gown; its skirt beautifully fans out at the bottom. I choose my jewelry with precision. Great earrings made of purple mother-of-pearl, and a necklace of black pearls. Around my wrists I wear bracelets made of cowry shells. My hair is tied up in a large bun on the top of my head and is bound with a shawl in sea-colors.

I enter into the room, where the others are waiting. I embrace everyone in a greeting. Then I sit down and concentrate on what I wish to tell.

"Thank you all for coming. First of all, I want to give you some additional information about the symbolism of your rings called the Lapis Sancti Magi. These rings connect your inner world with what happens in your life. What are the consequences of this? You will have figured out by now that the Lapis Sancti Magi causes a magical space in your life, a 'Garden for the Soul' that makes it easier to sow and harvest new things in your life. The effects of these changes kept you busy for the last few months!

"On top of this you all have been thoroughly tested. That is normal when you are influenced by the Old Tradition. The Inner Worlds test you on power and motivation, to see whether you are ripe to proceed along the Golden Path, to determine whether you are ready for the next step. You can only proceed when your inner-self is strong enough to take the full responsibility for what is yet to come.

"The first test that you underwent was the Test of Earth. It was followed by those of Water, Fire, and Air. Now you are facing a new trial: The Trial of the Spirit of the Deep. This is an important test!

"Realize that our contemporary society is facing a huge crisis, and the character of this crisis is not only economical in nature. The Spirit of the Deep wants us to understand this struggle as a conflict within the nature of every human being. You have gained consciousness of the struggle for power, the tug of war about truth and of the pollution of the Earth on all levels."

I look at Jason and say: "You quest for the cause of the crisis and the discovery of the disposable truth was a great step in your awakening process.

"It is of the utmost importance that you research the conflict within your own soul. Only then your ego can die, only then you will become one with your Mythological Hero."

I see eyebrows rising in question marks. I look at Lucas and say, "Do you remember your question about your life's mission and the myth that you are living? All of you who are present, you are the archetypical hero in your life! All of you have a mission to accomplish. Let's compare ourselves with the Greek myth of the Argonauts, that mythological ship with the fifty heroes aboard."

"Then, we will need to find a few more," Gabriella jokes.

"It is clear who I am," Jason says. "Melusine, I will carry you to the other side of the canal at the opposite side of the street, while I put one of my shoes on my head," he exclaims jokingly.[17]

I turn towards Jason while squeezing my eyes and say, "Be careful what you wish for, you might get it…"

I concentrate on the topic. I look around and search for eye contact with everyone. "Only when you connect yourself with your archetypical hero, you can begin to play an effective role in the greater matrix by spreading goodness and strengthening value and virtues in this world.

"Thus, Jason, as a journalist you are connected with the archetypical writer and use the power of your pen. Lucas, you as a farmer search for the collaboration with the Planetary Deva, in your professional field of agriculture. Gabriella, as a nurse you will probably find your calling in care. It is useless when spiritual people escape into the New Age world out of discontent and develop into the next generation of well-meaning healers working in poverty from an attic room; the Great Magical Work can only succeed when everyone starts to add the essential spiritual core to their own profession!"

---

[17] The Ship of Stars

I point to the eye in the stone of the ring: "One Eye in a Triangle. But how is this eye created? The One Eye comes into being by the melting together of the Two Eyes. The Two Eyes of the Spirit of Eternity are the Sun and the Moon.

"The Sun symbolizes waking consciousness; the Moon stands for the ability to reflect, to withdraw your awareness deep inside and to contact the sub-consciousness. The deeper you withdraw, the more you will penetrate into the Collective Sub-consciousness.

"When your activities in the world are calibrated to your contemplation in your inner world, you perform the 'Holy Marriage.' This is a Western spiritual term that equals the Eastern word 'enlightenment.' It is also called the 'Hieros Gamos,' or the 'Unification of the Two Lands.'"

"The most important thing you need to know is that this 'marriage' is about the union of two parts of your soul! The Sun is your waking self; the Moon symbolizes your Inner Guide, who is of the opposite gender."

"That is very interesting," Lucas answers. "The picture becomes clearer to me. But how to work with these concepts?"

"You need to Awaken the Sleepers and Ignite the Interior Stars," I answer.

Awaken the Sleepers!

"The higher parts of your soul are asleep. In mythology they are often pictured as 'Sleepers.' The image of the Sleepers is very ancient. You already find it in the oldest Egyptian literature, in the Book of the Night. You also find them in fairy tales, like Sleeping Beauty and Snow-white. These soul parts can be awakened by poetical consciousness, and by using your imagination. The initiates of the past called fantasy an 'ass,' a headstrong animal tending to go its own way. But it is pulling forward the Arc of the Covenant, the most sacred treasure of the world!

To awaken these higher parts of the soul, the psyche needs to develop a spiritual relationship with the world of fantasy. When you apply this technique the right way, you will get visions.

"How does a vision arise? In your daily life you collect knowledge and life experience. When you start to work with the fantasy images of the ancient sages – the talismanic images – a relation between their essence and your life experiences starts to grow. Slowly they melt together, and when that happens you get intensive realizations, breakthrough moments. In one elongated moment of intensity a peak experience fills your consciousness with meaning. In that timeless second, that feels like hours, one image looms up that contains everything. All the former images and experiences clench into one image, outside of linear time... and deifies. That is the reality of Mystical Awareness, a part of Transpersonal Consciousness. You find examples in ancient Mediaeval and Renaissance art, in paintings like the Splendor Solis

or the pictures by Hildegard von Bingen. These types of images are the western equivalent of mandalas. By travelling in the imagination into the inner worlds of these images, you might enter into the same experience as the artist who made it had. This experience extends 'normal synchronicity,' the type of coincidences where you open a book and find the answer to that question in life that you are wrestling with. The experience of a vision is life changing in one second.
"Teresa of Ávila describes this in her work *The Interior Castle*:

"There are people in whom the imagination is so ill, the ratio works so hard, or for other reasons that they believe they see everything they think.
When they would have had a genuine vision, they would know without doubt that they were wrong, because their imagination is not followed through by an effect. They stay cold, and it is as quickly forgotten as a dream. This is not the case with a real vision. The soul is deeply emerged in thoughts and completely not occupied with seeing things. Then suddenly the vision appears. A huge fear, awe, a mix of strong emotions fills all the senses, and meanwhile they are enclosed by a silence. In the Inner World arises a gigantic movement and everything quietens down quickly. The soul has learned such a fundamental truth that she does not need a teacher."

All attendees are making notes. I give some space to the group to process the information and to ask questions. It remains difficult for people to imagine this information when they haven't gone through the experience yet.

It is time to have a break and drink some coffee. The group is quiet; everyone appears to be deep in thought. I think it is all too new, too fresh, it needs to sink in.

Then the chatter starts and the group exchanges their daily experiences. Jason tells about his visit to the summer carnival. He paints the folk event in colors and scents. He talks about the rhythms of the samba and his passion for dancing.
"I became so emerged in that dance, that I lost Rudolph and Robin at a certain moment," he chuckles.
"What was her name?" Wolf asks.
"Ehh, what do you mean?" Jason asks thoughtfully.
"What was the name of the reason that you lost Rudolph and Robin on the way?"
Jason looks at him smilingly and gives him a friendly poke. "You are no longer allowed to guess. Her name is Salomé."
"Beautiful name," Wolf answers. "How does she look?"
"She has long black hair and she was wearing a transparent dress made of organza, in the colors of the rainbow. We danced, drank a few beers, flirted and kissed. On top of that we have made an appointment to get to know each other better."
I react with goose skin, rub my arms and try to collect the images that appear before my inner eye.
Then I ask everyone to take their seats again and investigate what kind of associations they have as a reaction to my story.
Gabriella is very emotional. "That story of the Hieros Gamos: it reminds me of that awful experience, when Fiona 'initiated' my Gerard into spirituality! That serpent claimed to be a priestess and tried to lure my Gerard into an extramarital affair! I am still so

angry and resentful that someone is capable to take things so completely out of context. She was talking about 'spiritual sex' and invited Gerard to participate in some kinky sex ritual.

"He would play the role of the God, and she herself would – as a priestess - take on the part of the Goddess. She held out a sexual energy of a type that I was unable to give him at home. Fiona was able to manipulate him so viciously! She told him that she was an anointed priestess of the mysteries and claimed to have access to wisdom of the past. That suggests an authority! At home I told my story. About the subconscious female part of your own soul, about the goddess that lives deep inside of yourself. But the story that I had to tell was of course not so exiting as the seductive strategy of Fiona. I am still trying to get my mind around what truly happened there. Was it recalcitrant behavior? The refusal to be constrained?"

It is clear that the crisis this other woman caused in her marriage still hurts Gabriella.

"The Sacred Marriage is symbolic language for the melting together of two parts of your own soul," I emphasize. "The type of temptation that Gerard was exposed to by Fiona can cause severe wounds and incapacitate people for a long while to proceed further on the path. They overlook an important principle, and that causes them to act from desire and mix up inner and outer levels. Love and passion; both come forth from the God Eros, but they are two completely different forces. In the Middle Ages they talked about 'Minne,' a higher form of love that was not meant to be consumed, but caused the development of the noblest characteristics in someone. When you mix up Minne and desire, you get trapped in a charm and pay a heavy price.

"This theme is depicted in the Dance of the Seven Veils. The Goddess – the archetypical feminine – reveals her beauty. During a whirling seducing dance she drops her veils, one by one. That is symbolic language. The Goddess reveals herself to the soul of a man in the form of the Dancing Beauty. Carl Gustav Jung called her the Anima and regarded her to be one of the parts of the soul from the Collective Unconscious mind. She is the part of the inner psyche that perfects the male psyche. Women have a comparable subconscious male part of the soul: the Animus. His esoteric title is the Beloved, or the Bridegroom. According to Jung, every human being has characteristics of both of the sexes, in the biological, as well as in the psychological sense.

"Every veil of the Dancing Beauty depicts a layer of his female side, and while She reveals herself to him, She shows even more of Her beauty. During his life he is unable to see Her in her full nakedness, because the last veil that covers Her is symbolic for the passage between life and death.

"Symbolic language connects you with the Collective Unconsciousness; it is hidden behind all events and is timeless. Step through the symbol and you enter into the world of the living experience that it represents, and you become a prophet. As a prophet you perceive things differently. The Kundalini energy will rise steady and controlled. The energy flow in your neurological system increases like a rising snake. That is what they call the 'Shaman's Disease.' By the contact with the Spirit of the Deep, the Metanoia deepens. In this experience, present, past, and future, melt together and time pales.

"The average person scan their minds to find solutions for the problems of every day. But when you perceive past, present, and future as one, you see the essence, the primal pattern of the events in which you are involved, before they become disguised by the influence of time. In this deep layer of the Collective Unconsciousness all the events of the entire world are still in their seed-condition. It is after the seeds 'touch the earth' that they start to take root and germinate. Ever repeating desires and experiences follow the same pattern and they become charged by feelings of hope and fear. For your spiritual development, it is of the utmost importance to bring your soul to the point where time is no longer a limiting factor.[xvii] The meditation training brings you to that timeless level. To that end we use our Transpersonal techniques.

"Do you recognize it, that you try to solve your problems with the help of your personality? Do you buy self-consciousness by emphasizing your looks? Do you try to win the rat race by relying on status? You try to compensate what has lost its balance. Instead of building confidence, you buy an expensive suit; you 'take' a beautiful girlfriend, or repair a faltering relation with a child. But compensation is in fact misbalance by definition, a misbalance that you try to fix by putting another misbalance at the other side of the scales. Compensation does not solve anything. It doesn't get you out of trouble; it does not lift you to a higher level."

The attendees look at each other and then they look back at me with questioning eyes. Lucas asks the question that is hovering in the air. "But, what is the solution to develop yourself?'

Ignite your Interior Stars!

I look at them and answer, "You need to learn to 'Constellate.'" Again, questioning faces. Everyone listens attentively. "Constellation is willfully applied imagination. The word i-magi-nation comes from magic. By means of Constellation you consciously create an Internal Cosmos by means of your imagination. In this internal universe you consciously give a place to all the parts of your soul.

"Most people compensate their shortcomings, their incompetency, or their blockages. As I have said previously, there is only one problem with that coping strategy; it does not work! A depressive mood does not go away by changing your facial expression, or by eating chocolate. A midlife crisis does not disappear by changing partners.

"The last few months you have all been busy with the 'laying out of a garden' in your soul. That garden works like a mandala. At the four sides are the places of the Four Elements; Earth, Fire, Water, and Air; each have gotten their own area. The garden is surrounded, protected by the Golden Ring, that is symbolic language for the path that the Sun travels around the Earth; a symbol for your higher consciousness. By the division of your psyche into the Four Elements, you have also generated a free space in the middle of your garden. This is the place for 'Spirit,' for the Divine, the Transcendent. By Constellating you create a Heaven in your consciousness. You do that my means of systematic meditations."

I take a felt-tip pen and make notes on a whiteboard that stands in the classroom, to make clear what the successive steps are:

- *Learn to acknowledge the many facets of your soul.*
- *Then recognize them in daily objects and during daily activities.*
- *Link these parts of your soul systematically and deliberately to the Talismanic Thoughtforms that represent these different soul parts.*

"You do this by creating peak experiences wherein you connect the symbols with the appropriate emotions. This technique equals the creation of talismanic images and Ushabti's."

- *When you link peak experiences to the different parts of your soul, the Sleepers will wake up;*

"In other words, the sleeping parts of your soul become contacted. Then they become the 'Interior Stars', because these images change into divine visions. These start to give off light and start to radiate!"

"Let me give you an example, because I see that it is difficult. One of these Interior Stars is the Planet Venus. Venus is a symbol for all erotic love relationships. That is why the Magical Image of Venus is a beautiful naked woman."

"The peak experiences that belong to this image are all flirts, petting-parties, orgasms that you have ever experienced during your life."

"The everyday experience is the erotic love connection with your own partner. You start to work by making a conscious connection between your partner, your erotic peak experiences, and the Goddess Venus."

"The I-magi-nation, the Magical Image of the Goddess Venus - a beautiful naked woman – does not only contain your *personal* peak experiences, but she is built up from the peak experiences of all the people that have ever lived. Can you imagine how much energy is gathered in this Talismanic Image? It is divine. The greatness and the awe that this Magical Image starts to generate, when this part of your soul awakens, causes a radiance that washes through you. Your erotic experiences get a supernatural glow, because with the awakening comes a power that is in no way comparable with a 'normal' erotic experience. Your soul will contact the Magical Image of the Goddess Venus during the contact with your partner. That is what is meant by the term 'Ignite the Interior Stars.' These awakened parts of your soul become fires of endless possibilities and of eternal joy!"

"Through Constellation you install these inner patterns consciously. Hereby you equip your soul with an infrastructure. You create imaginative environments that are especially designed for the soul. Constellating is inner work; it is done through meditation, mystery play, and ritual. Due to this you cause the different parts of your soul to awaken and to take their appropriate places in your consciousness, and thus in your life."

Everyone is silent. Lucas sighs audible. An undefinable atmosphere of expectation and of hope hangs in the room! It is as if we all together fell into that timeless unity. It is a similar atmosphere that can also be invoked through ritual. Even speaking about these topics and explaining them, connecting with these ancient old teachings, frees the soul. The music that is softly playing in the background now switches. I hear the tones of a classical era; the 'Song to the Moon,' from the opera Rusalka. I smile when I recognize the song of the mermaid and think, *Everything perfectly develops in synchronicity.*

Then I continue my explanation. "At this moment in your training you have accomplished the most important classification of your psyche: the realms of Earth, Fire, Water, and Air. Now the time is ripe to work with Spirit, with Mindpower. Start with connecting the Four Elements to their Talismanic Images; connect Earth to the Winged Bull, Fire to the Winged Lion, Water to the Eagle, and Air to the Winged Human Being. These four constellations are connected to the tests that you have passed at this point in time.

"What you need to do now is to learn to 'Accommodate.' Accommodation is the third psychological process. When the Four Winged Beings support you from the inside, you start to connect their Talismanic Images to the most common daily events. Classify your daily experiences first of all by the Four Elements, and you will already build on another type of relation to reality. Later in the process you start working with the other Astral Images of the Zodiac. Instead of connecting your energy fully to the material plane, you will now start to provide the Planetary Deva with what she is entitled to get. Adapt your lifestyle in such a way that you are in harmony with the Planetary Deva!"

"The transforming power of growth whereof I speak does not come from the earth, but from the life giving spirit inside. If the earth would be abandoned by her Planetary Deva, she would die, and with her all life on earth..."[xviii]

"Start to build bridges between the material world and the fertile ideas of the human mind. These bridges connect the material plane with the spiritual world and with the Minne-energy of the God Eros." I look at Gabriella and put my hand gently on her arm. "Gabriella, that is why your Gerard became confused.

"In the Middle Ages nobility also worked with these spiritual powers, courtly love was called Minne. It is a gigantic love power that builds the bridge between this world and the Otherworld based on the bitter sweet longing for a love that cannot be consumed, Minne is not earthed!

"Of course all this is a form of applied psychology. The terms Constellating and Accommodating talk about what needs to be done to build and work with the 'Heaven Inside.' Within that Internal Heaven the parts of your soul move. They are embodied by the classical planets: Sun, Moon, Mercury, Venus, Mars, Jupiter, and Saturn. In the Hermetic Mystery Tradition they are called the 'Interior Stars.' They correspond with the deeply felt movements of the soul. They are no part of your personality. Mars is not simply your anger, and Venus is no imprisonment in bodily awareness. The planetary parts of the soul are deeply anchored in your psyche. They generate many complexes, fantasies, and behavior. The Heaven-Inside is as vast and as endless as the heaven outside. The Internal Planets are as mysterious, massive, and alien as the planets outside. When you awaken the Sleepers, the sleeping parts of your soul, you connect them with the classical planets in your Inner Heaven. Then the Interior Stars inflame!"

"The Interior Stars are gorgeous Talismanic Images, great archetypes, magical mandala's, imaginations of soul parts. In the Collective Unconsciousness they have merged into Gods and Angels, they have grown into enormous fields of consciousness and knowledge, perfected by the experiences of many generations of priest-magicians. Because of their perfection we can attune to their frequency and they give direction to our transformations."

"Make yourselves ready for a challenge, because all of you have developed yourself in spirituality and are now at the point of your training where you will shortly get involved in the Test of Spirit. Be aware that you can only take on the Great Work when your inner world is strong enough to withstand the pressure."

Then I rise and close the meeting. I need to reflect and prepare myself because the climax of the Great Magical Working is at hand. *Has the preparation been sufficient? It will get critical with this new factor, Jason's amorousness.* I walk through all the steps, there is nothing left to do than pray and work...

Ora et Labora

After the meeting Jason walks over the cobbles back to his car. It is still early in the evening. He looks at his telephone and discovers a series of messages from Salomé. She has tried to call him. He decides to answer her quickly, because she is unaware of the fact that he has been unattainable this afternoon. Luckily she picks up the phone.

"Sorry for being unreachable," Jason excuses himself. "I was in a closed meeting this afternoon. It is finished now; I can come to your place if you would appreciate that."

Salomé understands and is very happy that he has answered her messages. Jason hears her friendly laughing on the other side of the telephone.

"Are you hungry? I just wanted to start cooking and I have enough food for an extra plate," she says. "It is no haute cuisine, but simply healthy food."

She does not need to say this twice. It has been so long ago that he had diner in a homely environment, together with a woman. And he is curious to get to know her better.

"I am on my way," he answers enthusiastically.

It is the beginning of a fantastic evening. She greets him happily. She looks awesome, bright shiny eyes, beautifully shaped, everything has the right proportions. Her black hair she has tied together with some Spanish combs. They greet with a warm kiss, shy... Salomé bends her head, stares at the ground and blushes from excitement. Jason walks in and looks around. Her house has been decorated beautifully and stylish, eccentric, in a style that he does not know. Lots of wood, copper, and stained glass. Furniture in an old style, carefully restored. The copper fittings of strange looking instruments carefully polished. A table of walnut in the center, chairs covered with velvet. A desk with a moss green tabletop. Lamps in Jugendstil. He stands still at a strange looking device, some mechanism with numbers engraved in it, and he recognizes astrological signs. The objects are entirely made out of brass.

"What is this?"

"It is an Astrolabe," she answers, "an ancient instrument to measure time by the position of the stars."

He looks around admiring. "Does this style have a name?"

"It is called Steampunk," Salomé smiles. "Along with being an interior style it is also a beautiful fashion style; large gowns, with a lot of lace and layers combined with tight earth wires."

They talk animated. Salomé tells about her profession as a game-developer. About her great passion for dance and her fascination for mediaeval festivals. She loves fantasy and re-enactment; everything comes forth from her fascination for ancient cultures.

Before long there will be a Celtic festival and her costume is ready for use. This time she will go as a mediaeval noblewoman. Proudly, she shows her costume: a gorgeous ornament on the head, made of a transparent shawl of black silk, adorned with silver spangles. The shawl is fastened with a beautiful silvery moon symbol that stands out on top of the head, like a Spanish comb. The veil falls down over her hair, down her back, and reaches the ankles. The costume comes with a tight lace earth wire and a skirt dressed up with tingling belly dance bells. It is put together from different colored organza, in the colors of the rainbow. Elegant shoes finish the costume.

"That will fit you beautifully," Jason says. "I would want to see you wearing this costume."

The evening is cozy and the food delicious, the wine tastes heavenly, as well as her sweet kisses. "When do we meet again?" After some searching for dates in the different schedules they end up with an appointment the next Friday, the start of the Celtic festival.

They look each other deep in the eyes and their souls melt together. The farewell at the door is sensual. Jason kisses her lips and she answers enthusiastically. Her skin feels as soft as velvet and Jason clearly feels her nails in his upper arms when his mouth explores her long neck. He travels her throat with his lips and is joyful when a soft cry escapes her. He embraces her tighter while he looks at her. He feels her breasts pushing against his chest. He strokes her hair and says, "Then let us make our appointment in the early evening, and visit the festival. Later that evening I have a planned meeting with a closed group. I cannot change that appointment."

It is the only possibility to meet at a short notice in two full schedules, so they agree to meet at the festival. "I will try to find a fitting costume for this occasion," Jason smiles. Humming, he walks to his car and when he steps in, he feels those butterflies again that he did not experience for a long time.

Throughout the week a lot of text messages go to and fro, and in between they speak several times on Skype. Over the course of the week Jason tries his best to find fitting Celtic clothing for the event. Eagle offers a solution. He has a nice costume, the suit of a mediaeval magician consisting of leather trousers, and a white mediaeval shirt that is completed by a hooded cape.

"You can keep it on for our meeting afterwards on the beach," Eagle remarks, "because we will meet in ritual robes there."

"That is very practical," Jason exclaims enthusiastically, "I won't lose time by changing cloths."

Eagle is happy for Jason. He tries to dig up who Salomé is and Jason dwells on how beautiful she is, how interesting, about her sense of humor, and her hobbies.

"Well, chap, I think you are madly in love," Eagle laughs.

The Spirit of the Deep

In my temple I prepare the regalia that we need for the outdoor ritual. My thoughts go back to that event, now almost thirty-five years ago. To the temple in the Otherworld. The sounding of the gong, the charging of the ring, the powers that came together on that altar, and Tethys, who conducted the Great Magical Working. In my mind I hear Tethys voice again, *"People need to reawaken for the Otherworld to live and work from their spirituality. Let us summon these Powers on the Inner Planes."* I hear her arguing in the temple to reawaken a Solar Hero that can inflame the Earthlight:

Sleeping priestesses, dormant mages,
Dreaming in the Eternal Sea,
In the starry shining Oceans of Light,
Dreaming of a golden heaven with a honey colored firmament
Awaken, wake up!

I recall the forging of the Lapis Sancti Magi by Wolf and Michael in the volcanic fires of Mount Atlas. The memories of this Great Ritual of Power still move me deeply. I clearly recall the moment when I was standing next to the central altar and took the responsibility on me; to connect my work for the Gods, tie it together with this particular ring, and to train the one who would find it. In my memory I relive the moment, wherein the powers came free and swirled. I clearly remember how I collected these energies. In a great vortex they whirled over the altar. With the Force of the Lightning flash I consecrated them into the Lapis Sancti Magi, and thus this particular ring became a living talisman. Then I put the golden ring in its protective box and threw it into the Astral Sea. Together we watched how it fell; it was caught by the waves. The beautiful ring drifted across the waves of the Sea of Stars, until it was no longer visible. It had disappeared into the Deep.

This ritual was followed by the Temple Sleep. In my lucid dreams I searched where I needed to go, in order to fulfill my task. I was thrown out from the heavens. It was as if I was gliding down in a huge waterfall, sliding downwards on the whirling waters. On my way down, I saw landscapes, magical realities. I glided deeper and deeper and searched for the beginning. Is it even lower? I fell, until I arrived at the spiritual level where I could reach the people that I needed for my task. Then I found myself back in London and woke up in a body in the room in the conference center, where we were working that very weekend.

We are almost full circle now. The powers are drawing together and the moon is nearly full. I always come with a mission. I incarnate when there is a great need for the renewal of the connection with the Light of the World. People identify with the archetype that I represent. Like some of my colleagues I will probably not be able to escape the fate to slowly and gradually rise as a star and be worshipped as a Goddess.

I incarnate in this time, when the pureness of nature is gradually blemished and the dignity of humanity is in danger, their calling and truth are increasingly damaged. My origin is the Deep, Tep Zepi.

I am a member of the Old Family Lefay, the eldest daughter of Tethys and Titurel. We Lefays are the old Grail-family. We are always expected to come. Our origin is the Land of Joy at the other side of the Eternal Sea.

I was born before Time, in the Seas of Dreams on the Waves of Enchantment. I came swimming from the Land of the Youth. I crossed stormy seas, and went through the great Portals of Time. I come when it is ebb and when old magic is needed to restore the balance.

Some folks believe that we Lefays stem from Egypt or from Sumer, but those cultures did not even exist in those times. I was no longer young, not even in those days.

Behind the visible world, great forces are active. Forces that determine the Spirit of the Time. They are great waves of consciousness. They determine what is fashionable; they inspire new inventions and the ever changing landscape of cultural heritage. The Spirit of the Time is comparable with the waves of the Eternal Sea that come ashore as frothy crests. Like the pattern of air bubbles of sea foam, thus the Spirit of the Time brings primal patterns to the earth that will germinate in the world. Primordial patterns that cause friction and thus, cause development:

> *Fertility and Sterility,*
> *Wisdom and Folly,*
> *Dominance and Surrender,*
> *War and Peace,*
> *Wealth and Poverty,*
> *Beauty and Decay,*
> *Life and Death ...*

Further ahead in the Ocean of Eternity, the waves become increasingly higher and their powers multiply. Cosmic consciousness equals the Waves of the Sea. The Sea flows out over the Land and brings new ideas and events to manifest in the World of Time. They are comparable with sea foam. But the most powerful waves come from the Deep, they determine the alluvion. They bring the influence of the Spirit of the Deep, the Deep Consciousness of the Cosmic Ocean.

"We, who incarnate, work closely together with the forces of this Deep Sea. We always come with a mission, and that is to accomplish a change in the Spirit of the Time....

I change my clothes and dress myself in my sea-green gown, made of woven seaweed. I put a collar of black pearls around my neck and earrings of mother of pearl in my ears. I adorn my wrists with cowry shells and put my feet in elegant slippers. Then I take the regalia and carefully lay them in my basket, woven from seagrass. I take a last look in the mirror, raise the collar of my robe and hang my blue green cape with hood around my shoulders. Then I fasten my trumpet shell at the belt around my waist and leave my house to prepare the ritual at the beach.

*****

Hand in hand, Jason and Salomé explore the festival grounds. They admire the stalls, swing on the rhythm of the music of a Celtic band and drink a glass of wine in one of the tents. They stroll through the complex while they share their impressions. Jason sets his alarm clock as a reminder of the time that he needs to leave. He reminds Salomé of the appointment with the group. He will meet up with them at the visitor's center at the edge of the Drowned Land. As they sit down on the grass they tease each other, then playfully frolic around until the time that Jason's alarm bell goes off. He says goodbye to Salomé with a warm embrace, an intimate kiss, and an appointment to meet each other soon. Salomé watches Jason; she admires his appearance while he slowly disappears in the masses.

When Salomé rises she sees a wallet on the floor. She picks it up, hesitating as she decides to open it to see who the owner is. Then she reads it is Jason's. It must have fallen out of his pocket while they were playing. *What to do?* She tries to call him, but apparently he has switched off his cell. *One cannot travel without money? What if he needs gas on the road? I will try to catch him.*

Salomé passes through the crowd and walks to the exit, she overlooks the parking area. It is packed with cars, and even the surrounding roads are full of cars that have been parked at the road banking's. *What next?* She walks the long road to find her own car, steps in and decides to make a tour of the parking area. Jason is nowhere to be found. *How far from here would that visitor's center be?* Her navigation shows her that it is only a fifteen minute drive away. That means that she has one chance left to deliver his wallet, and that is to drive to the center in the hope that she finds him there. She types the address in the GPS and hits the road in the direction of the cost.

*****

While I walk towards the chosen spot, I leave a trace of burning tea lights that work on batteries, so that everyone can find the right spot without problems. I walk over the plank bridge, in the direction of the tidal. I search my way along the quicksand, along the mud-flats and straight through bubbling streamlets. The tide is exactly as planned and the moon slowly rises, imposing over the wad. I walk to the place of the Sea Altar that is straight at the coastal line of the Westerschelde. It is made from a large piece of driftwood. I decorate the altar with the regalia I brought with me. I carefully lay down the trumpet shell, and after that I start to draw a large magical circle in the ground with my staff. It is getting dark quickly now and the first stars appear at the firmament. I look back and see the trace of small lights running through the wilderness. It is a grandiose sight. When I am ready I see the first lantern dancing towards me. I try to see who it is. I think it is Michael. One by one the others arrive. Gabriella, Wolf, Lucas, Leo, Eagle, and as lastly, in a hurry, Jason arrives.

All are dressed in floating robes with hooded capes. With dancing lanterns in their hands they walk through a moonlit landscape.

"Thank you all for coming to this ritual which is of the utmost importance. Tonight is the night that all forces will be anchored, and this will cause people to wake up for the needs of the planet. The Thoughtform which we will be creating this evening will spread itself telepathically through the population. By this ritual a Constellating factor will be anchored, and implemented in the Spirit of the Time. Through this the people will become aware of the Earthlight again and restart to maintain it."

I notice that everyone is very concentrated. Eagle breathes deeply, Gabriella straightens her back; Jason releases all the tension of his hasty journey, by moving his neck and shoulder muscles. I look at everyone, search for eye contact, and see that they are all attentive and ready to proceed.

Together we place our burning lanterns at the sea altar. I start with the ritual invocations for the work of this evening:

O House of Stars, adorned with Lapis Lazuli Blue
Oh holy city, called Atlantis,
Founded on a dais in the Cosmic Ocean,
Cathedral built for the rites of Magicians and Priests,

> *House wherein the incantations for Heaven and Earth resound.*
> *The Watchtower of the North burns bright;*
> *Winged Human Being, ignite your beacon,*
> *We are ready and join our forces!*

I look up and see the beautiful heaven in a clear sky, gradually filled with stars. I take the trumpet shell and blow it. The sound echoes over the sea.

> *Winged Human Being, we are waiting for your essence,*
> *Incarnate at the altar!*

We all look up in expectation, and clearly see a shooting star in the northern heaven ... the light flashes downwards. Jason's aura lights up against the evening sky. An unearthly light starts to radiate from him, and he appears to grow energetically.

Lucas carefully carries a green glass to the sea altar and puts it down. Michael ignites a specially consecrated candle, thus a beautiful green earthlight burns on the sea altar, amidst of the Drowned Land. Gabriella carries the chalice with seawater and I sense the altar. All elements are present: the Earth level is now completely aligned with the Supernatural. Together we intone the next incantation:

> *O House of Stars, adorned with Lapis Lazuli Blue,*
> *The Winged Human Being is standing at the altar,*

We call for the arrival of the Bride of the Cosmos!

I put my bracelets with the cowry shells on the altar and ask the participants for their full concentration. For the second time I take the trumpet shell and blow it. While the sounds still echo over the sea, the noise of running feet approach over the wooden planking and Salomé looms up from the darkness.

"I am so sorry to disturb you folks, Jason; you have lost your wallet!"

Jason turns around, bewildered he sees her standing in the full moonlight, still dressed in her gown of rainbow colored veils. The huge silver crescent moon towering over her head. Jason does not know how to feel right now: this rough interruption of the sacred atmosphere makes him feel ashamed. But because of her appearance and her radiance his full amorousness burns loose.

Salomé is confused as well. She looks around and an understanding breaks through. She speaks purely from intuition, pulled along by the magic of the moonlit scene, by the enchantment of the group all dressed in ritual robes, and the pure beauty of the scene. "I have looked for you all my life, where were you?"

I embrace her and kiss her on both cheeks and say: "How wonderful that you have found us, my daughter. We are always here, in all generations. We are happy that you have arrived just in time, because we have sought you as well. Be welcome! People, greet your sister, welcome her in our House of Light."

What happens next can only be explained by the magic of that moment, wherein the archetypical forces gather together and the enchantment dawns. On the rushing sounds of the sea, the Dance of Eternity arises. On the enchantment of Eros and the waves of desire, Salomé intuitively does what she does best; she dances! She dances the Dance of the World. In the Magical Circle of the Four Elements she dances the dance of the Dancing Beauty, who is the Bride of the Cosmos, and discloses one by one the secrets of the Goddess. Wolf resounds the singing bowl that I brought along, Eagle recites the text:

> *Jason Adams, what is the secret of the Winged Human Being?*
> *That human... that is you!*
> *Look to the Goddess of Life*
> *She reveals her first secret...*

And Salomé dances! On the rhythm of the sea, waving on the rhythm of the tides, and as if completely natural she loosens the yellow veil from her costume and starts a serpentine dance in the light of the moon:

> *The firs Interior Star that she ignites in you,*
> *Reveals the Secret of the Sun:*
> *In the Land of Duality this star flares up.*

> *When you transcend your first dilemma:*
> *Do you choose a life of sterility, or of fertility?*

Another beat of the singing bowl, Lucas and Gabriella speak together:

> *The second Interior Star reveals her next secret;*
> *The Secret of the Moon.*
> *When the Bride of the Cosmos drops her second veil,*
> *She challenges you with the dilemma of Wisdom and Folly.*
> *But this madness is nothing more than the fever of the Metanoia,*
> *The rising force of the snake Kundalini,*
> *awakens in you the Dream of the Shaman*
> *and you hear the Voice of the Spirit of the Deep:*
> *Winged Human Being, is there a place in your heart for Magic?*

Salomé dances, the tingling bells of her gorgeous costume resemble raindrops on the water. Now she takes her silver veil from her skirts and whirls around in the middle of the circle, around the sea altar, her bare feet dancing in the sand. Again the singing bowl vibrates, followed by the voices of Leo and Wolf:

> *Her third Interior Star is Mercury.*
> *When she ignites this light and drops her third veil,*
> *She asks you whether you are prepared to fight for what is right;*
> *Winged Human Being, do you take the lead over your circumstances,*
> *Or are you being led by them?*

Salomé takes her orange veil and now walks towards Jason. She teases him, flirts, attracts him, and pushes him away. Jason answers, at first carefully, the he lets himself go in the enchantment. The next gong beat, Gabriella and Lucas ask Jason and Salomé:

> *The fourth Shining Light of the Goddess is Mars.*
> *When she drops her red veil*
> *She gives you a dilemma;*
> *Are you willing to fight for Inner Peace?*

Salomé takes her red veil and runs straight towards Jason. She jumps forward at him and lands with her chest against his. Wolf and Michael recite the next piece:

> *The Goddess illuminates her fifth Interior Star;*
> *Her fifth secret is hidden in Jupiter.*
> *When She drops her blue veil, she crowns you!*
> *She gives you the keys to Wealth and Poverty.*
> *How do you rule your Inner Kingdom, Jason?*
> *Do you cultivate it, do your rule it?*
> *Or do you let your spirit be overgrown by despair and fear?*

Salomé takes her cobalt blue veil from her skirts and hangs it around Jason's shoulders, like the mantle of a king. She takes a rock from the sand and puts it in his hand as if it is an orb. She takes the staff from the altar and hands it over as his scepter. Lucas and Gabriella continue the spell:

> *The sixth Starry Light is the Light of the Goddess Venus:*
> *When she drops her green veil,*
> *She reveals her beauty.*
> *Jason, Winged Human Being;*
> *Are you capable of perceiving the Beauty of the Goddess?*
> *Or do you turn down her attraction,*
> *degrade her powers and change her into a prostitute?*
> *Jason, the Beauty of the Dancing Beauty*
> *Equals the beauty of the Goddess as she lives inside of you.*

Salomé now faces Jason, she is vulnerable. The only things she wears are the black veil that covers her hair and face, the earth wire of her costume, and a beautiful string. The great moon symbol on her forehead reflects the light of the full moon.

I step forward and look at the couple. "Six of the Veils of the Goddess belong to this world. They are there for you to enjoy, they reveal themselves in you mutual love, in Eros, in Minne. Within a long-lasting relationship, during a lifetime, the love of men and women is consumed. During that time a man can Constellate his wife and identify her with the Goddess. During that time a woman can Constellate her husband, and connect him to the Inner Planes. Through this mutual act, both will grow in inner beauty, in power, and in mission."

"However, the Goddess holds a last secret, and that secret does not belong to this world. When you fill your life with meaning and love, when you continuously try to live in harmony with the Spirit of the Deep, she will reveal her eternal face to you. It is time to disclose her last secret."

Become enchanted by that Beauty,
That reveals itself in life and death!

I raise my arms and spread them out towards the full moon; I encircle the Sea Altar three times and resonate my words over the water:

We gather our forces.
The time is ripe to awaken the Planetary Deva.
She floats Between the Worlds as a Sleeping Beauty
On the waves of the Eternal Sea.

I take the trumpet shell once more, and for the third time the echoing sound of the shell bellows over the waters. We all watch in awe how a wooden ship comes sailing towards us. The sails are up, and on the fabric is painted a red rose. The ship moors at the eastern side of the magical circle.

Jason opens his eyes wide, brings his hand for his mouth; he realizes that he has dreamt this recently!

I gesture the company to follow me. We walk along the gangway. I watch the phenomena appearing in nature around me. The High Hour approaches, there is only a moment of time left....

I lead the company to the cabin and gently open the door. There she lies; Dindrane, the naked Sleeping Beauty, exactly as Jason saw her in his dream, amidst a bed of soft smelling roses. The Lady of the Planetary Deva, within her arms lies the antique sword with the pelican on the scabbard. Cautiously, everyone gathers around her.

"You can only see the Goddess naked when you have access to the Otherworld."

The Seventh Interior Star is Saturn,
In this Light, the Goddess holds the Mystery of Life and Death.

I look around me. "You are standing at crossroads, where just a few living people get access. The only living beings that are exceptionally allowed to look behind this veil are the priest-magicians and shamans of this world. The dividing line between these worlds is too compressed, but for priest-magicians this purple veil is thin, and they are allowed to pass at certain times. They know that what is being born on Earth dies in the Heavens. And that which dies in this world is being born in the Heavens. In between these worlds, the priest-magician is the Walker-between-the-Worlds. That is the secret of the Initiate of the Temple. The bridge between these worlds is made from the voice of the Spirit of the Deep, the Holy Spirit."

Jason steps forward, takes the envelope, and slides the letter out. He unfolds the paper and reads:

> *"You who sets foot in this sacred place;*
> *Assure yourself that you see me for what I am.*
>
> *I am your Inner Trust,*
> *Your loyalty to your sacred mission.*
>
> *When you no longer confide in me,*
> *I will leave you and I can no longer help you.*
> *But when you fill yourself*
> *With the full passion for your Sacred Work,*
> *I will enflame in your heart*
> *And illuminate the world wherein you live."* [xix]

I look at Jason and Salomé and say: "The Sacred Marriage is conducted when the outer world and the Inner Worlds are one. Behind the Dancing Beauty stands Dindrane, Lady of the Planetary Deva. It is time to wake her up."

Jason bends forward and kisses Dindrane on her eyelids. Dindrane opens her eyes and slowly sits upright. Carefully Michael takes over her sword and helps her rise from the bed. He leads her to the throne standing at the high end of the cabin.

Dignified she sits on the High Chair, an example of beauty and health. She is crowned with a fabulous crown of roses in her red hair. With one hand she lifts the sword. The pelican on the sword starts to bleed. Salomé steps forward to help her and offers Dindrane a white handkerchief. Dindrane takes it and with it she wipes off the blood from the sword. She returns it to Salomé: three drops of blood decorate the white surface.

Then Dindrane opens her other hand, which she holds at heart level. She shows a ring, the Lapis Sancti Magi. She closes her fist again and brings her forefinger to her mouth in a gesture of silence.

She reopens her hand. "The Lapis Sancti Magi is the ring of the Initiates, Jason. You now know the meaning of all the symbols that are engraved in it. But there is one determining factor lacking: give me your hand."
Dindrane shoves the ring onto to Jason's finger. "You yourself are the center of your golden magical circle, Jason. Ora et Labora, pray and work; knowing that we are intimately connected to each other. Be in love, let yourself be seduced and enchanted by the Dancing Beauty. Realize that I speak through her as your own soul. I am you Anima, the Planetary Deva who lives Between-the-Worlds, in all the hearts where love resides." Then Dindrane rises from her chair and hands me her sword. "Lady, it is now up to you."

The Mystery of the Sea

We leave the ship that floats in between the worlds. There is a last secret that needs to be disclosed. I lead the companionship back to the Sea Altar. I feel that the tides are at the point of switching.

"Our work is almost done, the blessing of the Spirit of the Deep rests upon you all. The consciousness for the Planetary Deva has been aroused, the Earthlight has been reawakened. The physical and the spiritual are one!"

Then I feel the energies switch, the moment that I have been waiting for. Enormous powers awaken in my spine. I loosen my hair so that it fans out over my breasts and my back. I detach from my personality. I am aware of the stars above my head and identify them as my crown...."

Jason, Salomé, and the initiates now see the tide rising, the land slowly drowns into the sea. The Sea Altar becomes completely surrounded by water, the Moon is full. The Venusian Powers of the Friday turn over into the Saturnal forces of the Saturday, and the company witnesses how Melusine changes...

Her two legs change into two fishtails, while she takes on her true shape of the Fay Melusine, the Lady of the Lake.

The company of initiates stands at the shore and everyone looks in amazement how the Constellation takes places. The robes of

Melusine, woven from seaweed dissolve in the seawater. Melusine generates by her energy a gigantic Sphere of Sensation that illuminates the entire landscape with electrical fire. Because of the charged air also Jason notices his powers rising.

Jason Adams, man of the Earth, the powers now also rise within him. The entire scene swells into a roar, the intensity becomes cosmic. The Fay opposes the archetypical Human.

The company witnesses how Melusine grows in height. They see how the constellation Pisces appears in the night sky. It melts together with Melusine's double fishtail. The two beaks of the constellation meat at the place of her vulva, they interlace and thus form the Vesica Pisces: a gateway to the Cosmic Deep. Powers flash in enormous lightning over the landscape. Melusine still holds the sword that Dindrane kept safe for her. Her voice thunders over the waves when she addresses Jason:

"Jason, Re-Member the powers of this sword. Its name is 'The Memory of the Blood'. This is the sword of your cultural ancestors. Continue this night with a vigil at the beach and contemplate your inheritance. Be conscious of the fact that your heart is forged in their Living Light."

A lightning flash illuminates the beach when Jason takes the sword from Melusine's hands. Then Melusine swells into cosmic proportions. Above her head the North Pole stars radiate and form a diadem. The full moon at her left side changes into her mirror. In her other hand she holds a comb. She combs her hair, so that these will shine as beautiful rays when her face melts together with rising sun at the upcoming Golden Dawn.

At the sea altar, in the Drowned Land, Jason and Salomé stand in an embrace. They look upwards. Jason lifts the sword in a greeting. The initiates now become overshadowed by the four Holy Beings in the clouds, they surround Melusine Lefay. She raises her arms in a blessing gesture, and her voice echoes over the landscape:

Lux Orta Est,
The Light has risen!
I stand guard and watch the Sacred Lands
As I have done in the past and will continue to do in all Times to come,
For I am eternal and I will never die.

Then she finishes her transformation and folds her fishtails; knots them together above her head, so that she is surrounded by a perfect circle.
Through the opening of the Vesica Pisces the boat with Dindrane sails back into the Otherworld and even then Melusine grows further… until she has become one with the Milky Way.

*****

From behind her veils
Tethys waters her gardens,
From the foam she weaves Her robes
While it contracts into solid matter,
Her face remains calm and serene.

How to proceed?

When this book gave you appetite to taste more, you can start to practice the exercises in the book:

1. The Great Kabbalistic Cross
2. The Primordial Hill meditation.
3. The Water Spells
4. With a little help from my book 'The Temple of High Magic' you can practice the creation of a magical circle.
5. With a group from four to nine people you can perform the ritual that is included in this book and thus charge your own magical ring.
6. For questions you can reach me on my Facebook page. There I will announce all the practical courses for people who want to proceed.
7. You can also apply for the training courses which will be announced through my Facebook, newsletters, and websites.
8. When you are a high sensitive person, or when you notice the awakening of Kundalini power in you, you can contact me for help and advice.

Ina Custers van Bergen

Trainer Transpersonal Development

Ancient western traditions teach methods that have been passed down through the ages, either by mouth-to-ear; from teacher to student. Step-by-step you contact even deeper layers of your Self.

Ina Custers was trained as a teacher within such a classical tradition, the Hermetic Mystery Tradition. Besides well-known institutions for Transpersonal Development, she has worked for years within psychic healthcare. She is a certified sociotherapist, hypnotherapist, NLP and Timeline therapists, and also a Regression therapist. Ina is a Reiki Master and was trained in Systemic Therapy and Family Constellations.

She specializes in the Hermetic Mystery Tradition. To her, the mythological roots of Western Culture form fundaments of Transpersonal Development. To this end she draws from ancient Mediaeval and Renaissance sources, as well as Hermetical writings, Greek Mythology, Egyptian Magic, as well as Arthur legends, Alchemy, Ceremonial Magic, Jewish Kabbala, Tarot, Angelology, and Arabic Astrology.

Ina is the head of the Hermetic Order of the Temple of Starlight, a mystery school that aims at reconnecting modern people to ancient wisdom teachings, to help people generate peak experiences that generate significant insights and form the fundaments for ethical self-development. She develops study courses for the order, and publishes books and articles.

Ina Custers lectures, organizes retreats, workshops, and training throughout Europe. The methods she uses cause life changing experiences and include meditation, prayer, mystery play and ritual drama, methods that have been used since antiquity to raise consciousness.

For more information and trainings in the Hermetic Mystery Tradition, you can contact the Hermetic Order of the Temple of Starlight where Ina Custers van Bergen is the Director of Studies.

www.templeofstarlight.eu
info@templeofstarlight.eu

It is possible to work with Ina Custers van Bergen in an individual basis through Skype.

You can also order colored posters of the art in this book. at www.themysteryofthesea.com

Transpersonal Training

The Quest for Alchemical Gold

Transpersonal Training puts you into contact with your inner authority, the place from where you build your life. This core of yourself is a source of inspiration, the source of your values. It is here where the mission of your life wells up.

By building a conscious relation with this core, you enable yourself to be authentic and congruent in all circumstances of life. By means of Transpersonal Training you let go of limiting patterns of the past and you enable yourself to renew your energy and transform your qualities, thus bringing them to a higher level.

The Temple of High Magic

Hermetic Initiations in the Western Mystery Tradition

Ina Cüsters-van Bergen

ISBN 978-159477308-2

Before the advent of Christianity, early civilizations had, at the heart of their spiritual traditions, Mystery schools that offered a corpus of training methods in what is now called magic. The persecution of heresies that followed the establishment of Christianity as Rome's state religion, a persecution that reached its high point during the Middle Ages, forced the degradation and disappearance of this training system. While the knowledge of these Mystery traditions--jealously guarded by secret societies--has begun to emerge, the actual techniques and practices of spiritual magic have remained hidden.

The Temple of High Magic provides the practical knowledge of these techniques for modern spiritual seekers who wish to incorporate the proven esoteric techniques of the magi into their lives. This book explains the dynamics of group ritual and solo practice, as well as the critical role played by the Kabbalistic Tree of Life--the key to inner knowledge. Ina Cüsters-van Bergen shows that temples of high magic are not mere physical structures but are the inner edifices willed into being by a sustained meditative practice and Pathworking, by using key symbols from ancient Hebraic and Egyptian traditions. Sometimes called the Yoga of the West, this spiritual magic is a system of esoteric development that seeks to create full union between the magician and the divine.

The Solo Magical Training

Magic the Basics
The Elements of the Wise

Ina Cüsters-van Bergen

Know yourself, discover your abilities. That is the biggest challenge. The Solo Magical Training guides you, in 50 steps, and every lesson a tangible goal: study, experience, implement and internalize.

Each lesson and every topic is a new building block of what will become your Interior Temple. Abilities disclose, realizations clear up, senses sharpen, all elements balance.

It is your personal journey of development with the Kabbalistic Tree as your guideline and Ina Custers van Bergen as your guide. You walk under supervision the 'Path of the Snake,' a journey that will ask everything from you: endurance, creativity, and transpersonal development. It returns even more; energy, focus, insight, and the power to be and to change.

References

i	Carl Gustav Jung.
ii	Free translation of Marsilio Ficino De Vita Triplici.
iii	Free translation of Giovanni Pico della Mirandola, Oration on the dignity of man.
iv	Free translation of Marsilio Ficino De Vita Triplici.
v	Free translation of Marsilio Ficino De Vita Triplici.
vi	Free translation of Giovanni Pico della Mirandola Oration on the Dignity of Man.
vii	Inspired by The Ancient Egyptian Coffin Texts Volume 1 Spells 1-354 R.O. Faulkner spell 353.
viii	Inspired by: The Egyptian Book of the Dead, the Book of Going Forth by Day, The Theban Recension, spell 57.
ix	Lucebert.
x	Inspired by: Lancelot – Grail. The Old French Arthurian Vulgate and Post-Vulgate in Translation. Vol. 2 The Story of Merlin, translated by Rupert T. Pickens page 34.
xi	The Red Book, Carl Gustav Jung.
xii	Inspired by: Lancelot – Grail. The Old French Arthurian Vulgate and Post-Vulgate in Translation. Vol. 2 The Story of Merlin, translated by Rupert T. Pickens page 34.
xiii	Inspired by "The Winged Bull", Dion Fortune.
xiv	Stenographica Trithemiigenuafascilis, dilucidaquedeclaratio.
xv	Trithemius Antipalus, lib. II, cap. 3, pp 326-27 en lib. III, p. 390.
xvi	*The Chemical Wedding of Christian Rosenkreutz.*

xvii	Inspired by; *Marsilio Ficino Theologia Platonica de immortalitate animae.*
xviii	Inspired by; *Basil Valentine Lemmi Classical Deities.*
xix	Inspired by; *Lancelot-Grail, Volume 6 The Quest for the Holy Grail, the Old French Arthurian Vulgate and Post-Vulgate in Translation. Translated by E. Jane Burns.*